AIRCRAFT ACCIDENT REPORT

Air Accidents Investigation Branch

Department of Transport

Report on the accident to Sikorsky S-61N, G-BEID 29 nm north east of Sumburgh, Shetland Isles on 13 July 1988

LONDON: HMSO

© Crown copyright 1990
First published 1990

ISBN 0 11 550983 6

LIST OF RECENT AIRCRAFT ACCIDENT REPORTS ISSUED BY AIR ACCIDENTS INVESTIGATION BRANCH

1/89	Airmiss between Tristar G-BBAH and Tupolev 154 LZ-BTE near Lydd, Kent on 6 February 1988	February 1989
2/89	Incident involving BAC 1-11 G-AYWB and Boeing 737 EI-BTZ at Gatwick Airport on 12 April 1988	May 1989
3/89	Sikorsky S61N helicopter G-BDII near Handa Island off the north-west coast of Scotland on 17 October 1988	June 1989
4/89	Boeing 747 N605PE at Gatwick Airport on 1 February 1988	August 1989
5/89	Boeing 747-136 G-AWNM on approach to Runway 27L at London (Heathrow) Airport on 11 September 1988	December 1989
6/89	Concorde 102 G-BOAF over the Tasman Sea, about 140 nm east of Sydney, Australia on 12 April 1989	December 1989
1/90	Sikorsky S61N G-BDES in the North Sea, 90 nm north-east of Aberdeen on 10 November 1988	May 1990
2/90	Boeing 747-121, N739PA at Lockerbie, Dumfriesshire, Scotland on 21 December 1988	
3/90	Sikorsky S61N, G-BEID 29 nm north east of Sumburgh, Shetland Isles on 13 July 1988	

Department of Transport
Air Accidents Investigation Branch
Royal Aerospace Establishment
Farnborough
Hants GU14 6TD

9 August 1990

The Right Honourable Cecil Parkinson
Secretary of State for Transport

Sir,

I have the honour to submit the report by Mr E J Trimble, an Inspector of Accidents, on the accident to Sikorsky S61N, G-BEID which occurred in the North Sea 29 nautical miles north east of Sumburgh on 13 July 1988.

I have the honour to be
Sir
Your obedient servant

D A COOPER
Chief Inspector of Air Accidents

Contents				Page
	GLOSSARY OF ABBREVIATIONS			(vii)
	SYNOPSIS			1
1.	FACTUAL INFORMATION			2
1.1	History of flight			2
	1.1.1	Flight and ditching		2
	1.1.2	Evacuation		3
	1.1.3	Rescue		4
1.2	Injuries to persons			5
1.3	Damage to aircraft			5
1.4	Other damage			5
1.5	Personnel information			6
1.6	Aircraft information			6
	1.6.1	Leading particulars		6
	1.6.2	General description		7
		1.6.2.1	Aircraft	7
		1.6.2.2	Powerplants	7
		1.6.2.3	Drive train	9
		1.6.2.4	Main gearbox bay	10
		1.6.2.5	Rotor brake	11
		1.6.2.6	Fire protection	12
		1.6.2.7	Flotation and emergency equipment	13
		1.6.2.8	Lifehatch	14
		1.6.2.9	ADELT	14
	1.6.3	Condition monitoring		15
		1.6.3.1	Vibration	15
		1.6.3.2	Engine oil system	16
	1.6.4	Maintenance		17
		1.6.4.1	General	17
		1.6.4.2	Maintenance history	17
		1.6.4.3	No 2 powerplant and drive train	19
1.7	Meteorological information			19
1.8	Aids to navigation			20
1.9	Communications			20
1.10	Aerodrome and approved facilities			20
1.11	Flight recorders			20
1.12	Examination of wreckage			22
	1.12.1	Recovery		22
	1.12.2	General		23
	1.12.3	No 2 engine		23
	1.12.4	No 2 drive train		25
	1.12.5	Main gearbox bay		26
	1.12.6	Lifehatch		27
	1.12.7	ADELT		27

1.13	Medical and pathological information		27
1.14	Fire		27
1.15	Survival aspects		28
	1.15.1	Flotation equipment	28
	1.15.2	Evacuation management	28
	1.15.3	Lifehatch	29
	1.15.4	ADELT	29
1.16	Tests and research		30
	1.16.1	Engine No. 5 bearing	30
	1.16.2	Clearance between Thomas coupling and EMRSA	30
	1.16.3	IDS tests	31
	1.16.4	Previous cases	32
	1.16.5	Rotor brake	34
	1.16.6	Firewalls	34
	1.16.7	Lifehatch	34
	1.16.8	MGB oil pipeline	35
	1.16.9	Fuel pressure transmitter hoses	35
1.17	Additional Information		35
	1.17.1	Engine Fire in Flight Drill	35
	1.17.2	Crew immersion suits	36
2	**ANALYSIS**		37
2.1	Conduct of the flight		37
2.2	Evacuation		38
2.3	No 2 Powerplant power turbine and drive train		41
	2.3.1	Cause of power turbine and drive train damage	41
	2.3.2	Cause of No. 5 bearing failure	42
	2.3.3	Cause of No. 5 bearing cage failure	43
	2.3.4	Cause of No. 5 bearing overload	44
	2.3.5	Cause of Thomas coupling distortion	46
	2.3.6	Vibration monitoring	47
	2.3.7	General health monitoring	48
2.4	Fire		48
	2.4.1	Initiation of the fire	48
	2.4.2	Progression of the fire	50
	2.4.3	Firewalls	51
	2.4.4	Fire protection	51
2.5	Rotor brake		52
3.	**CONCLUSIONS**		53
	(a)	Findings	53
	(b)	Cause	54
4.	**SAFETY RECOMMENDATIONS**		55

APPENDICES:

1   Aircraft General Layout
2   Powerplant and Main Gearbox Layout
3   Power Turbine Layout
4   Drive Train Layout
5   Rotor brake assembly
6   Rotor brake deficiencies

GLOSSARY OF ABBREVIATIONS

ADELT	-	Automatically Deployable Location Transmitter
AMM	-	Aircraft Maintenance Manual
amsl		Above mean sea level
ATC	-	Air Traffic Control
BIH	-	British International Helicopters
CAA	-	Civil Aviation Authority
CVR	-	Cockpit Voice Recorder
DP	-	Dynamic Positioning
DSV	-	Diving Support Vessel
EMRSA	-	Engine Mounting Rear Support Assembly
FCU	-	Fuel Control Unit
FDR	-	Flight Data Recorder
GRP	-	Glass Reinforced Plastic
HRc	-	Hardness, Rockwell Scale C
Hz		Hertz (cycles per second)
IDS	-	Input Drive Shaft
IEVC	-	Installed Engine Vibration Check
IP		Input Pinion
JAR	-	Joint Airworthiness Requirements
km		Kilometre(s)
kt		Knot(s)
MCD	-	Magnetic Chip Detector
MGB	-	Main Gearbox
MHz	-	Mega Hertz
mm	-	Milli meters
Nr	-	Main Rotor Rotational Speed
OD	-	Outside Diameter
PA	-	Public Address
PN	-	Part Number
PT	-	Power Turbine
PX	-	Pressure Transmitter
ROV	-	Remotely Operated Vehicle
rpm	-	Revolutions per minute
RTF	-	Radio Telephony
SN	-	Serial Number
SOAP	-	Spectrometric Oil Analysis Programme
TSN	-	Time Since New
UHF	-	Ultra High Frequency
USG	-	United States Gallon
UTC	-	Coordinated Universal Time
VHF	-	Very High Frequency
VFR	-	Visual Flight Rules

SIKORSKY S61N

G-BEID APPROXIMATELY 45 MINUTES AFTER DITCHING

Air Accidents Investigation Branch

Aircraft Accident Report No: 3/90
(EW/C1077)

Registered Owner and Operator:		British International Helicopters (BIH) Ltd
Aircraft	*Type:*	Sikorsky
	Model:	S-61N
	Nationality:	British
	Registration:	G-BEID
Place of Accident:		In the North Sea, 29 nm north east of Sumburgh, Shetland Is. Latitude 60° 17'N, Longitude 000° 44'W
Date and Time:		13 July 1988 at 1431 hrs
		All times in this report are UTC

SYNOPSIS

The accident was notified to the Air Accidents Investigation Branch by the Shetland Marine Rescue Sub-Centre at 1505 hrs on 13 July 1988 and an investigation began the same day. The AAIB team comprised Mr E J Trimble (Investigator in Charge), Mr A N Cable (Engineering), Mr D J Mearns (Operations) and Mr P F Sheppard (Cockpit Voice Recorder).

Whilst operating a passenger flight from a North Sea rig to Sumburgh, the crew heard an unusual noise which was almost immediately followed by a fire warning on No 2 engine, and shortly thereafter by a fire warning on No 1 engine. Three minutes after the initial noise a controlled ditching was carried out 11 nm from the Shetland Island coast onto an almost calm sea. By this time the cabin had filled with smoke. All twenty one occupants evacuated successfully into liferafts and were winched into a Search and Rescue helicopter. After a fierce fire had consumed much of the floating aircraft, the remains broke up and sank.

The report concludes that the accident was caused by an uncontrollable fire in the main gearbox bay which probably resulted from the effects of failure of the No 5 bearing in the No 2 engine. An underlying factor was the lack of any fire detection or suppression capability within the main gearbox bay. The cause of the bearing failure could not be positively established.

Twenty-seven Safety Recommendations were made during the course of the investigation.

1 FACTUAL INFORMATION

1.1 History of flight

1.1.1 Flight and ditching

The helicopter G-BEID (ID) departed the Safe Felicia, a North Sea semi-submersible rig, at 1345 hrs with two pilots and a full passenger load of nineteen for a one hour charter return flight over the North Sea to Sumburgh. No cabin attendant was required by regulations for the flight and none was carried. At 1423 hrs, when 40 nm from Sumburgh and 15 nm from the Shetland Island coast, cruising on Track 'J' at 1500 feet altitude in Instrument Meteorological Conditions (IMC), ID established radio telephony (RTF) contact with Sumburgh Approach Air Traffic Control (ATC), which identified the aircraft on radar and passed an inbound Visual Flight Rules (VFR) clearance.

The co-pilot, who was the handling pilot, reported that 5 minutes later he heard a muffled crack or "bang". This was also heard by a number of passengers, and in particular by the occupant of seat No 4B (Appendix 1), as a loud bang from above, from the area of the No 2 engine drive train. The noise was not heard by the commander, but both crew felt that there was possibly a slight change in the vibratory "feel" of the aircraft. About 6 seconds later, while the crew were discussing this, the No 2 engine fire warning lights illuminated brightly. Engine instrument checks revealed nothing unusual and no signs of smoke or fire were observed by the crew. Passengers heard a number of abnormal noises after the bang, and the passenger in seat No 4B described a grinding mechanical noise, again from almost directly above.

After the fire warning the co-pilot started a descent and, in accordance with the drill: 'Engine Fire in Flight, Step A - Suspect Fire', the commander retarded the No 2 engine speed select lever to ground idle and started a stopwatch. He transmitted a Mayday distress call at 1428:44 hrs on the Sumburgh ATC Approach frequency, informing ATC that the aircraft had experienced an engine fire, in error identifying it as on No. 1, and that the intention was to descend to 500 feet and continue VFR. About 48 seconds after the bang, the No 2 engine was shut down by operation of the Fire Emergency Shut-Off Selector handle and the main fire extinguisher fired in accordance with Step B of the drill.

The No 2 engine fire warning lights remained illuminated and 90 seconds after the initial noise, while waiting the specified 30 second period before firing the reserve fire extinguisher, the No 1 engine fire warning lights also illuminated. The other engine indications remained normal. At about this time passengers saw oil coming from the cabin ceiling, streaking down trim panels and the inside of the left window adjacent to seat row No 4. The oil dripped almost continuously onto the occupants of seats No 4A and 5A. Oil covered the outside of the right windows at rows No 4 and 6. Smoke issued from a joint in the ceiling panels in the central part of the cabin.

The co-pilot increased the rate of descent, breaking cloud at 800 feet amsl, and levelled out at low height, assisted by the "check height" voice alerting audio warnings at 250 and 100 feet radar altimeter height, from the automatic Low Altitude Warning System. The commander, still without visual confirmation of fire, informed ATC that ID was "now showing fire on both engines continuing VFR towards the coast". He briefed the passengers via the cabin public address (PA) system to prepare for an emergency ditching, and took the aircraft controls. On the commander's instructions, the co-pilot deployed the floats and made a"ditching" RT call. The co-pilot put his head out of the cockpit window to check float deployment, saw a great deal of smoke behind and reported that the aircraft was on fire. A gentle power-on ditching was made 11 nm off the Shetland Island coast at 1431 hrs, some 30 seconds after the visual confirmation of the fire and 3 minutes after the initial abnormal noise.

1.1.2 Evacuation

After ditching, the co-pilot streamed the sea anchor and the aircraft floated satisfactorily with its flotation bags correctly deployed. The seawater-activated switch which should have stopped the Cockpit Voice Recorder (CVR) on ditching did not operate and the CVR continued to record for some five minutes after touchdown. The Automatically Deployable Emergency Location Transmitter (ADELT) was not manually activated by the crew and did not automatically deploy.

The commander shut down No 1 engine, instructed the co-pilot to open the cabin door, and attempted to apply the main rotor brake, but found that the normal resistance to brake lever operation was absent and the brake ineffective. A passenger in seat row No 4 saw the brake lever being pulled down and simultaneously heard an abnormal metallic grinding noise from an area corresponding to the rotor brake location. While the rotors were running down, the co-pilot entered the cabin, which was filling with wispy grey acrid smoke that was rapidly becoming more dense. He donned his immersion suit, opened the cargo door at the forward right side of the cabin and launched the forward liferaft. The commander did not don his immersion suit.

The commander remained in his seat while the rotors were running down, which took some 2 minutes, and during this time ordered the launching of the rear liferaft and the evacuation of the passengers. He then entered the cabin and found that he was unable to see through the smoke beyond seat row No 3. The crew became very concerned for the passengers in the rear seat rows, but the smoke had become so thick and nauseous that they were unable to penetrate to the back of the cabin. They were unable to find a crew smokehood or oxygen equipment, since none was stowed on the flight deck of this particular aircraft. There was oxygen equipment on board, but this was stowed under Row 8, near the aft end of the cabin. Meanwhile 6 passengers had gathered in the rear of the cabin and were attempting to manually jettison the lifehatch, which had not been remotely unlatched by cockpit action. They reportedly experienced considerable difficulty and delay in unlatching the lifehatch and removed an adjacent push-out window in an attempt to reach the external release handle. The passengers finally managed to jettison the lifehatch and launched and boarded the associated liferaft.

Some 4 minutes after ditching the passengers in the forward liferaft, which was still attached to the aircraft by its painter, who had initially seen small flames in the area around the No 2 engine exhaust, could now see signs of a growing fire at the right side of the main gearbox (MGB) housing. They exhorted the crew to leave the aircraft, which they promptly did. The two liferafts were paddled with difficulty away from the burning aircraft, linked together and the passengers redistributed to equalise the loads.

1.1.3 Rescue

On receipt of the distress message at 1428:44 hrs, Sumburgh Approach ATC immediately vectored a nearby S-61 (FK) towards the scene. At 1431 hrs, when Sumburgh Approach lost radar contact with ID, the crew of FK reported that they had just heard a ditching call. At 1433 hrs Shetland Maritime Rescue Sub-Centre (MRSC) scrambled an HM Coastguard S-61 SAR helicopter (Rescue 117) and requested that Aberdeen Maritime Rescue Co-ordination Centre (MRCC) scramble the Bell 212 SAR helicopter (Rescue 145) from the Cormorant Field. In addition, the Lerwick lifeboat was launched at 1445 hrs with an estimated time of arrival at the ditching position of 1545 hrs.

At 1435 hrs FK obtained a radar contact at 3 nm range, and shortly afterwards the crew sighted a plume of smoke. FK arrived overhead at 1436 hrs and reported that the helicopter was floating upright with liferafts deployed from the front and rear. Rescue 117 arrived on the scene at 1459 hrs, released FK to return to Sumburgh and commenced winching operations. After lifting 14 of the liferafts' occupants it was found necessary to dump fuel before lifting the remaining 7, which was accomplished by 1528 hrs. Rescue 145 arrived on the scene at about this time. Rescue 117 arrived at Sumburgh with ID's occupants at 1549 hrs.

1.2 Injuries to persons

Injuries	Crew	Passengers	Others
Fatal	-	-	-
Serious	-	-	-
Minor/None	2	19	-

1.3 Damage to aircraft

After ditching, ID drifted under the influence of tidal currents and wind with the fire growing. The fire spread within a few minutes into the cabin and about 15 minutes after touchdown the main rotor head and main transmission were seen to subside into the cabin. Approximately one hour after the ditching, when the fire had destroyed most of the fuselage structure above floor level, the remnants of the aircraft capsized and floated with only the tail boom above the sea surface. After an unknown period of flotation in this configuration, with the tail boom sustaining damage from a surface-borne fire, the fuselage remains parted at a position close to the attachment points of the main landing gear sponsons and the forward portion of fuselage sank to the seabed.

The aft portion of the fuselage continued drifting supported by the right sponson and associated flotation bag. The Lerwick lifeboat sighted the bag and commenced towing the sponson, it not being apparent initially that a large portion of the aircraft was suspended beneath it. After a short distance the aft fuselage remains broke away and sank, at position 60°17.32' N, 000° 44.8' W. After being towed for about a mile the sponson also sank, approximately 3 hours after the ditching. The sea depth over the area of the wreckage site was found to be between 90-110 metres.

Almost all the fuselage structure above the floor line was destroyed by fire, with the exception of the tailboom and the rear 2 metres of the cabin, the lifehatch and parts of the engine bay structure. Both engines, the main rotor head and main rotor blades had been damaged by heat but were generally intact. All components in the MGB bay were extensively heat-damaged; steel components such as gearwheels and generators had survived but the MGB casing had been totally consumed. All surviving parts of the aircraft had suffered prolonged immersion in sea water.

1.4 Other damage

None.

1.5 Personnel information

Commander: Male, aged 33
Licence: Airline Transport Pilot's Licence (Helicopters) valid until 1993
Helicopter type ratings: S-61N, Bell 47, AS 332L
Instrument rating: Renewed 24 February 1988
Medical certificate: Class I valid until 1 August 1988
Flying experience:

Total all types:	4778 hours
Total helicopters:	4658 hours
Total S-61N:	2855 hours
Total last 90 days:	203 hours

Duty time:

Off duty	8-10 June
10 hr duty period	11 June
8 hr duty period	12 June
10 hr duty period	13 June

Co-pilot: Male, aged 42
Licence: Air Transport Pilot's Licence (Helicopters) valid until 1989
Helicopter type ratings: S-61N, Bell 47, WS 553, AB206, BV 234
Instrument rating: Renewed 7 December 1987
Medical certificate: Class I valid until 1 August 1988
Flying Experience:

Total all types:	7335 hours
Total helicopters:	7225 hours
Total S-61N:	5960 hours
Total last 90 days:	221 hours

Duty time:

Off duty	9-10 June
10 hr duty period	11 June
11 hr duty period	12 June
11 hr duty period	13 June

Cabin Attendant: Not required and not carried.

1.6 Aircraft information

1.6.1 Leading particulars

Manufacturer:	Sikorsky Aircraft Corporation
Type:	S-61N
Constructor's Number:	61223
Year of Manufacture:	1964

Powerplant:	Two General Electric CT58-140-1 gas turboshafts
Certificate of Airworthiness:	Public Transport, valid until 26 January 1989
Total Airframe Hours:	23778 hrs
Hours since Last Check:	34 hrs
Maximum Authorised Weight:	20500 lb
Estimated Weight at Accident:	19426 lb
Centre of Gravity Range:	Within limits permitted by Operations Manual

1.6.2 General description

1.6.2.1 *Aircraft*

The S-61N is a twin-engined helicopter of conventional semi-monocoque aluminium alloy construction with a 5-bladed main rotor (Appendix 1). ID had 2 pilot seats and a 19 passenger seat cabin configuration. Fuel was carried in bladder cells below the cabin floor. The transmission was driven by the two engines, mounted forward of the MGB.

1.6.2.2 *Powerplants*

The two gas turbo-shaft engines were housed side-by-side in engine bays on the cabin roof (Appendix 2). A stainless steel section of the cabin roof formed the floor of the engine bays, with a titanium alloy centre firewall separating the two engine bays and a titanium alloy canted firewall separating each engine bay from the MGB bay. A forward glass reinforced polyester (GRP) cowl, and an aft cowl with an upper aluminium section and a lower titanium section, covered each engine bay.

Each engine consisted of a gas generator section which supplied combustion gases to drive a single stage free power turbine (PT) at a normal nominal operating speed of 18966 rpm. The steel PT rotor shaft was supported near its front and rear ends respectively (Appendix 3) by a roller bearing, No. 4 bearing, and a ball bearing, No. 5 bearing. The bearings were positioned at opposite ends of a cylindrical bearing support housing attached to the PT casing. Located on the PT shaft between the bearing inner rings (races) was a spacer and a worm gear sleeve, which provided a PT speed signal to the engine fuel control unit (FCU) via a right-angled drive assembly within the bearing support housing.

The PT shaft extended aft through a carbon rubbing oil seal at the rear of the PT module. This seal consisted of a static carbon ring in a carrier which was spring-loaded axially against a steel mating ring that rotated with the PT shaft. Both the carbon ring and the mating ring had fine tolerance mating surfaces, designed to be flat to within 3 helium wavebands.

The rear end of the PT shaft was formed into a three lobe-shaped section which mated with the socket of a polygon coupling, which transmitted the output drive from the PT. The polygon coupling flange incorporated a balance ring on its forward face, from which material could be removed for adjustment of dynamic balance. The polygon coupling, oil seal mating ring, No. 5 bearing inner ring and the spacer were sandwiched between the worm gear and a nut screwed onto the rear threaded portion of the shaft.

Bearing No. 5 (Part No. MRC 4003T47P01) provided axial constraint for the PT rotor and radial constraint for the aft end of its shaft, and consisted of 11 balls of 0.5625 inch diameter which ran on a static outer ring and a split inner ring which rotated with the PT shaft. The balls and both rings were of VCEP MHT high hardness steel (52100 steel modified with 1% aluminium, Rockwell C hardness (HRc) 58-62). The balls were housed in a silver-plated bronze cage, riding on the inner ring and normally rotating at around 38% of PT speed. Lubrication and cooling of this bearing was provided by an oil jet which was aligned to impinge on a chamfer on the forward outer radius of the inner ring. Normal operating temperature was reportedly in the order of 250-275°C. The normal loads reacted by this bearing were axial, - i.e. approximately 300 lb rearwards at cruise power, and 430 lb rearwards at Sea Level Take-off power.

The engine lubrication system was of the positive displacement, re-circulating, dry-sump type. A multi-element gerotor-type combined pressure and scavenge pump, fed from a reservoir tank, supplied pressurised oil at 20-60 psig via a filter to a manifold which ran alongside the engine. A branch line from the manifold supplied oil to three jets within the PT support housing, respectively spraying oil into No. 4 bearing, No. 5 bearing and the carbon rubbing seal. Used oil drained from the housing via a single scavenge pipe which incorporated a magnetic chip detector (MCD) and was returned by one element of the scavenge pump back to the tank. The three gas generator main bearings were similarly lubricated. Nominal engine total oil contents were approximately 4 United States gallons (USG) (Aeroshell Turbo Oil 500).

Each engine was mounted onto engine bay structure at its forward end by inboard and outboard mounts with vibration isolators, and mounted onto the MGB casing at its aft end by a tubular engine mounting rear support assembly (EMRSA). A flange at the forward end of the EMRSA was attached by studs to the aft face of the PT bearing support housing. A yoke at the aft end of the EMRSA (Appendix 4) was connected through an aft isolator, a magnesium alloy gimbal ring incorporating elastomeric vibration isolators, to a yoke bolted to the MGB input section casing. The EMRSA supported the rear end of the engine vertically, laterally and torsionally, the gimbal arrangement eliminating the transmission of any cantilever loads to the MGB casing. The EMRSA was steel, with a wall thickness of 0.08 inch and a nominal internal diameter of 4.56 inches, locally reduced by the bead of a circumferential weld to 4.50-4.52 inches and somewhat enlarged in the area of the forward flange. The joint between the EMRSA flange and the PT casing was not sealed.

An open 0.625 inch (16 mm) diameter hole was provided in the wall of each EMRSA, on the outboard side just aft of the flange, to allow in situ inspection of the Thomas coupling (para 1.6.2.3). A bracket for fitment of a vibration transducer was attached by two of the bearing support housing studs. Each EMRSA passed through a circular cut-out in the respective canted firewall with the gap between firewall and support tube filled by an annular fireseal, held against the firewall aft face by a bracket clamped to the EMRSA tube.

1.6.2.3 Drive train

The drive train from each engine was contained within the EMRSA tube and rotated at PT speed (Appendix 4). The flange of the PT polygon coupling was bolted at three positions, evenly spaced at 120° apart, through a triangular adapter to a Thomas flexible coupling, which consisted of a sandwich of 11 stainless steel annular leaves, each 0.0125 inches thick. Three further bolts, spaced mid-way between the polygon coupling/adapter bolts, connected the Thomas coupling to three flange ears formed on the input drive shaft (IDS, also known as the high speed shaft). Each bolt also carried a conical washer on either side of the coupling leaf sandwich. The Thomas coupling was designed to cater for up to 0.5° of continuous misalignment between PT and IDS axes, by flexure of the leaves between adjacent bolts. Nominal radial clearance between the Thomas coupling and the EMRSA was reportedly 0.131-0.150 inches (para 1.16.2).

A flange at the aft end of the IDS was attached, by four 'T' bolts, to the flange of a splined coupling which in turn was splined to an input pinion (IP) within the MGB. A register between the two flanges ensured radial alignment. The splined coupling was designed to cater for up to 0.5° of continuous misalignment between IDS and input pinion axes. It was a requirement that the 'T' bolt individual positions and orientations in the IDS flange holes were maintained on reassembly of the joint, and this was enabled by bolt head and IDS matchmarking. The associated nuts were weight-graded.

A limited duty "fall-back bearing" was provided by 4 composite pads bonded to the aft isolator aperture, to cater for loss of radial location of the rear end of the drive train. The pads had a normal radial clearance of 0.625 inches from the outer ring of the splined coupling and were intended to contain radial excursions of the splined coupling in the case of failure.

1.6.2.4   Main gearbox bay

The MGB bay structure on the cabin roof comprised a number of aluminium alloy and GRP fairings. That region of the bay within the 'vee' of the firewalls was covered by part of the engine aft cowls. A GRP drip pan formed part of the floor of the bay and was intended to collect fluid leakage from the main gearbox and associated systems. The drip pan was drained by three integral stub pipes per side, connected to flexible hoses which passed through the cabin to overboard drain points in the lower fuselage. A tube containing pitot-static lines passed vertically through a cut-out in the pan, the gap being closed by an elastomeric boot. The floor at the forward extremity of the bay, in the vee formed by the canted firewalls, was at a lower level, forming in effect a sump in this region which was drained overboard by a 0.25 inch diameter hole in each MGB bay sidewall. The EMRSA was open at its rear end and the whole of the annular space between its internal surface and the IDS, up to the power turbine casing, thus constituted part of the MGB bay.

The MGB housed within the bay provided support and drive speed reduction (main rotor 100% nominal speed was 203 rpm) for the main rotor, and incorporated an aft take-off for tail rotor and accessory drive, in addition to a forward take-off for the rotor brake. The generators, hydraulic pumps and hydraulic reservoirs were installed on the aft side of the MGB.

Each input pinion within the MGB input section was carried on an integral shaft with a forward and an aft flame-plated journal, each running in a plain white metal (lead-tin-copper alloy) lined bearing cup, at PT speed. The gearshaft was sealed to the MGB casing by a carbon rubbing oil seal. The drive from each pinion was transmitted through a roller/ramp input freewheel unit to a combining gearshaft (nominal 100% speed 3195 rpm), which drove the main epicyclic gear and also incorporated the rotor brake disc (para 1.6.2.5) on its forward end. Associated with each input free wheel unit was a hydraulic servo type torquemeter. All parts of the MGB casing, including mounting feet, were of magnesium alloy.

MGB lubrication and cooling was by a wet sump oil system, incorporating a main and an emergency system, with nominal total oil contents of 14 US gals (Exon Turbo Oil 274). Most of the external system was located towards the rear of the MGB, but the pressurised oil feed, (at a nominal 55-65 psi) was largely supplied by an external steel pipeline system. This included a 0.375 inch outside diameter (OD) pipe which was routed just forward of the rotor brake disc and supplied the No 2 torquemeter.

The MGB bay also housed a fuel pressure transmitter (PX) for each engine and associated fuel pipelines. Each transmitter was flexibly mounted on a bracket located on the aft face of the respective canted firewall and connected to a fuel line (pressurised at between 210-795 psig via a 0.04 inch diameter restrictor) from the engine-mounted FCU. Each fuel PX had a seal-leakage drain line that joined to an overboard drainage system in the engine bay. Each drain line also served an engine oil PX co-located with the fuel PX, and a nearby engine oil pressure switch. The bodies of the four PXs and two oil switches were of aluminium alloy. The four pipelines in the MGB bay each comprised a non-fireproof flexible hose, consisting of an elastomeric tube with an external steel braid of 8 mm outside diameter, running between a union on the PX and a union clamped in a cut-out in the canted firewall near its base. Within this vertical run on the aft side of the canted firewalls (a length of about 15 inches for the drain hoses and 22 inches for the fuel pressure hoses) the hoses passed close to the edge of a thin triangular titanium plate which was installed horizontally, as a stiffening gusset, in the 'vee' formed by the canted firewalls.

Specific arrangements for intermediate fixing of the fuel PX hoses between their unions were not contained in the Aircraft Manuals, although the aircraft manufacturer reported that standard practice required flexible hoses to be restrained at no more than 18 inch intervals. A number of British registered S-61N helicopters inspected in the course of the investigation exhibited different arrangements. In one case all four hoses were fixed to a bracket bolted to the stiffening gusset; in most cases each pressure hose was clamped only to its neighbouring drain hose about mid-way along the length.

1.6.2.5 *Rotor brake*

A Goodyear friction-type rotor brake (PN 9440345) was provided, which consisted of a 12.2 inch diameter steel disc (which rotated at 3195 rpm at 100% Nr) bolted to a flange on the forward end of the combining gearshaft. The brake disc was acted upon by a hydraulic twin caliper unit, which was bolted to the front of the MGB casing. A variable thickness shim, between the disc and the combining gearshaft flange, allowed for centralisation of the disc within the brake housing. Each caliper piston (Appendix 5) operated in a cylinder formed in the magnesium alloy brake unit housing, and carried a friction puck which comprised a disc of composite material cast onto a steel backing plate, with two protruding lugs. The backing plate was located on the piston by a raised rim formed around the face of the piston and was attached to it by two self-locking screws which passed through the lugs into holes in the piston rim.

Brake application was by hydraulic pressure generated manually in a master cylinder by operation of a rotor brake lever in the cockpit roof. The system, supplied from the auxiliary hydraulic system reservoir but otherwise separate from aircraft hydraulic systems, incorporated a pressure limiting relief valve (600±20 psig); an accumulator; a pressure switch to operate a cockpit central warning panel light when system pressure was above 10 psig; and passages within the master cylinder to dump system pressure when the cockpit lever was in the off position.

Each piston assembly incorporated a self-adjusting mechanism to compensate for wear and to maintain a minimum gap of 0.045 inch between the puck and the disc when the brake was off. A release spring located within a guide and acting between an adjustment ring screwed into the piston skirt and a mushroom-shaped self-adjusting pin, drove the piston away from the disc when the cylinder was depressurised, the pin head forming a retract stop for the piston. A friction grip installed in the brake housing held the pin and prevented it from moving towards the disc unless a certain force threshold, in excess of the capability of the retraction spring, was exceeded. This occurred on brake application if the gap between puck and disc was sufficient to allow elimination of the clearance between the spring guide and the pin head, in which case the pin would be dragged through the grip, thus restoring the required gap with brake released.

The operator's Operations Manual recommended that the brake be used when floating only if sudden exit were required, because of the yaw and roll reaction forces generated.

1.6.2.6 *Fire protection*

The engine bays, with their flammable fluid and potential ignition sources, were designated for design and certification purposes as firezones. They were separated from each other, and from the MGB, by firewalls and provided with fire detection and extinguishing systems. Such systems were not provided for the MGB bay and were not required by the applicable Airworthiness Regulations.

A fire detection sensing wire loop installed in each engine bay was mounted on the centre firewall, canted firewall and cowls on brackets intended to maintain the sensing wire clear of the mounting surfaces. Exposure of part of a sensing loop to temperatures above 301°C would cause a drop in electrical impedance sufficient to trigger a control unit, which would illuminate the appropriate (ENG 1 or ENG 2) red light on the Fire Warn Test Panel in the cockpit and a red light in the Fire Emergency Shut-off Selector Handle (also known as the 'T Handle' or 'T Bar') on the cockpit overhead control panel. The brightness of both of these lights was dependent directly on the temperature to which the sensing wire had been exposed and on the length of sensing wire exposed to the high temperature.

Operation of the T Handle for an engine would cause closure of the emergency fuel shut-off valve in the engine feed line just below the engine bays, and arm the engine bay extinguishing system. This used monobromotrifluoromethane agent fed to discharge tubes mounted on the centre firewall. The discharge systems for the two bays were interconnected to provide either a Main shot of extinguishant to each engine bay, or a Main and a Reserve shot to either bay. Relevant parts of the Engine Fire in Flight Drill in the BIH Abnormal/Emergency Checklist were as follows:

> STEP A - SUSPECT FIRE
> Speed lever   Ground Idle
> *If, after 30 seconds warning remains illuminated:-*
> Complete Step B - FIRE
> STEP B - FIRE
> *Signs of fire, with fire warning light illuminated.*
> Speed Levers   Fully Forward
> T Bar   Pull
> Fire Extinguisher Switch   Main
> *If after 30 seconds the fire warning light remains illuminated:*
> Fire Extinguisher Switch   Reserve
> *If positive signs of fire persist:*
> Land Immediately

1.6.2.7   Flotation and emergency equipment

The lower fuselage of the S-61N was sealed to form a watertight boat hull, and two sponsons, mounted by struts on either side of the fuselage, each incorporated a main landing gear leg and an inflatable flotation bag. The Ditching/Forced Landing Drill required the flotation equipment to be armed prior to touchdown and inflated by means of a cockpit Inflate Switch after ditching. A sea anchor, deployable from the cockpit to stream from the aircraft's nose, was fitted externally and was required by the Ditching Drill to be deployed with rotors running, if possible.

Modification No 061/56-00-014 had introduced the fitting of 11 push-out windows to the S-61N cabin, and each of these could be released from inside or outside by pulling a tab. Two 14 man Helirafts were carried in the S-61N cabin, one stowed near the forward cargo door and one in the Lifehatch (para 1.6.2.8). Each was provided with a long and a short painter, attached to the aircraft, and stowed on each of the two buoyancy rings was a knife for cutting the painters, in a transparent pocket, and two paddles.

1.6.2.8   *Lifehatch*

A lifehatch was incorporated on BIH S-61N aircraft in 1981/82 by BIH Modification No 061/25-61-023, and consisted of a jettisonable door which contained a liferaft. The lifehatch was located at the left/rear of the cabin. It was retained by four shoot-bolt latches that each located in a ferrule in the door frame and were linked by a system of rods and levers within the door. The latches could be operated by either an electric actuator mounted on the door, or manually by an external or a guarded internal handle. Manual unlatching of the door from inside was effected by removing a transparent cover over the handle and pulling the handle upwards. A placard with instructions to this effect was mounted alongside the handle. The electric actuator could be operated from an overhead panel in the cockpit by selecting first an Arm Switch, which armed the circuit and illuminated a circuit check caption, and then a Jettison Switch . Door unlatching was indicated by an Emergency Door Open light on the Master Caution Panel. The Arm Switch was required to be off for normal operations. Lifehatch jettison after unlatching should normally occur due to the weight of the lifehatch, particularly if waves caused the aircraft to roll, but in some cases a manual push could be required to dislodge it from the aperture. After jettisoning the lifehatch, the liferaft could be inflated and separated from the cover and door by a jerk on the associated painter.

1.6.2.9   *ADELT*

A modification was incorporated on BIH S-61N helicopters in 1987 to provide an Automatically Deployable Emergency Location Transmitter (ADELT), a buoy which contained an X-band radar transponder and a VHF/UHF transmitter that would emit homing signals when deployed. The ADELT was mounted in an external plinth located about midway up the right/rear sidewall of the fuselage and deployed by springs when released from a mechanical latch by an electrically fired explosive cartridge. The electrical source for the cartridge was originally a dedicated 12 volt lithium battery, but this had been removed from S-61Ns and the supply taken from an aircraft essential busbar. Cartridge activation could be initiated by any of three frangible switches, triggered by impact forces in a heavy touchdown situation; or by a saline switch in the plinth, operated by immersion in seawater; or by manual operation of a guarded Deploy Switch in the cockpit, with the ADELT Arm Switch in its normal in-flight 'Arm' position.

1.6.3 Condition monitoring

1.6.3.1 Vibration

Measures taken for the maintenance of a satisfactory standard of engine and drive train dynamic balance included the index marking of the components-stack on the PT shaft and of the IDS 'T' bolts, in order to enable reassembly in the same relative position after strip. During overhaul, there was also a requirement for rig dynamic balancing of individual components, and of the PT rotor assembly; the IDS complete with Thomas coupling assembly and 'T' bolts; and the input pinion. Maximum allowable imbalance was 0.2 gram-inch for the PT assembly, and 0.04 gram-inch for the IDS assembly.

Following engine reassembly, dynamic balancing runs on a vibration test ground rig were required, using a transducer designed to measure radial vibration and mounted on the bracket fixed at the forward end of the EMRSA (para 1.6.2.2). The procedure allowed repeat testing, after rotational repositioning of the polygon coupling on the PT shaft, in order to try to reduce measured vibration at the once/rev frequency to within a limit of 2 mils maximum "peak-to-peak" amplitude, at normal speed. When an acceptable, or best, polygon coupling position had been determined, the coupling and shaft were indexed to identify their relationship by scribing an '0' on the rim of the coupling flange, to correspond radially with an '0' stamped on the end face of the PT shaft, any previous inappropriate index marks on the coupling being crossed out. If necessary, measured vibration levels could be reduced to acceptable levels by removing material from the polygon coupling balance ring.

An Installed Engine Vibration Check (IEVC) was required by the Aircraft Maintenance Manual (AMM) in certain circumstances. For this check, the engine which was not under test was run at ground idle, while portable test equipment was used to measure the PT transducer vibration level on the other engine while driving the rotors. The basic criterion for this test was that the peak-to-peak amplitude of the PT once/rev frequency should not exceed 3 mils between 98-105% rotor speed. The procedure used to achieve this was to repeat the test with the IDS in different relative rotational orientations to the splined coupling until an acceptable vibration level was found in one of the four positions.

Two sets of circumstances in which an IEVC should be conducted were specified by the AMM. Section 1 of Chapter 71-1-0 (Feb 21/83) specified that "The check must be made after installation or reinstallation of an engine"; while Section 1A of a supplementary instruction (Rev 72 Jan 11/83), after stating that it "is to take precedence where it is at variance with the manual requirements" noted that "Each time an engine, engine aft support assembly, PT module and/or high speed shaft is replaced an engine vibration check must be carried out". The interpretation that ID's operator placed on the Manual was to follow the latter requirement, but not to specify an IEVC where an engine was removed for attention and then refitted in the same aircraft and position with the same IDS, provided that the relative rotational orientation of the IDS and the splined coupling was maintained, normally by means of indexing the components before disconnection.

An IEVC was not required by the Manual after replacement of a MGB but had, in fact, been conducted by ID's operator in these circumstances for a considerable period. However, at the end of 1985, after advice sought from the aircraft manufacturer confirmed the absence of such a requirement, the operator discontinued the check following MGB replacement.

The aircraft was not equipped for continuous monitoring of engine and drive train vibration levels, but the AMM included an Aircraft Vibration Check procedure (Chapter 18-10-00), instigated by the operator in 1981, which checked airframe vibration levels using portable test equipment and a cockpit mounted transducer. To conduct the check a permanent record was taken of the amplitude/frequency spectrum at a number of different flight conditions and compared with a table of acceptable levels. The AMM noted in regard to the check that the consequences of excessive vibration could be occupant fatigue and the possibility of mechanical fatigue failures, fastener loosening, frettage and chafing of pipes, cables, hoses and controls leading to failure, and increase in the failure rate of sensitive equipment. The AMM specified that "routine monitoring of vibration levels is therefore necessary", and scheduled the check as a routine item every 200 hours and, amongst other circumstances, following MGB or Main Drive Shaft removal/refitment or replacement. The check was not mandated by the CAA and the operator had discontinued it several years before the accident.

1.6.3.2 *Engine oil system*

The operator did not run a spectrometric oil analysis programme (SOAP) on the engines of its S-61N fleet, and there was no mandatory requirement for such a programme. No indication of oil system pressure filter blockage was provided. Cockpit engine oil system indications comprised a pressure and a temperature gauge, and a low pressure warning light. No cockpit indication of oil contents was provided.

The engine oil system incorporated four MCDs, including one in the No. 4 and 5 bearing combined scavenge line. Each MCD comprised a permanent magnet on a removable plug which was inserted into the oil flow path, and intended to attract magnetisable particles in the oil and retain them for inspection. No cockpit indication of MCD condition was provided. The operator conformed to an AMM requirement for MCD removal and visual inspection every 50 hours (P1 Check). No procedure was provided in the aircraft or engine maintenance publications which specified the required action in the event of finding debris on an MCD.

1.6.4 Maintenance

1.6.4.1 General

Records indicated that the aircraft had been maintained in accordance with an approved Maintenance Schedule (H5000, latest Issue 4). This required major inspection, overhaul or life limitation at the following flying hour intervals:

Engine Light Overhaul	-	2000 hours
Engine No. 5 bearing Scrap Life	-	6500 hours
Input Drive Shaft Inspection	-	2500 hours
Input Drive Shaft Overhaul	-	8000 hours
Main Gearbox Mid-Point Inspection	-	1500 hours
Main Gearbox Overhaul	-	3000 hours

For engine or MGB removal, the drive train was disconnected at the IDS/splined coupling 'T' bolts and the EMRSA at the gimbal. A powerplant was considered to comprise an engine, with IDS assembly and EMRSA attached. When the operator shipped a powerplant in this configuration, as was common, it was normal practice for plastic foam packing to be inserted between the IDS and EMRSA to provide radial support for the IDS aft end.

1.6.4.2 Maintenance history

The recorded operating hours for the aircraft and its relevant components at the time of the accident were as follows:

	Serial Number (SN)	Since New	Since Complete Overhaul	Since Light Overhaul	Since Mid-Point Inspection
Aircraft	61223	23778	-	-	-
Engine 1	280310	14009	7577	257	-
Engine 2	295223	11498	5573	1583	-
MGB	A14-1079	8859	1754	-	255
Eng 2 Bearing No 5	MOA T0499	4616	-	1583	-
IDS 2	90UA	8056	2043	-	727

The following events of possible relevance concerning the engines, drive train and MGB installed in ID at the time of the accident were indicated by the records:

DATE	ID TSN*	EVENT
16 May 86	-	Input Drive Shaft SN 90UA Overhaul.
Mar 87	-	Engine SN 295223 2nd Light Overhaul.
29 Oct 87	23051	Engine SN 295223 and Input Drive Shaft SN 90UA installed in No. 2 position of ID to replace units due for overhaul. Powerplant No. 2 last IEVC (Installed Engine Vibration Check) conducted.
28 Dec 87	23279	No. 2 Powerplant removed (to expedite change of Fuel Pump due for overhaul) and refitted. (No Powerplant No. 2 IEVC conducted.)
6 Apr 88	23523	MGB SN A14-1079 removed (for Mid-Point Inspection). Replacement MGB failed and SN A14-1079 refitted after Mid Point Inspection. Engine SN 280310 installed in No. 1 position following Light Overhaul.
20 April 88	23523	Powerplant No. 1 last IEVC conducted. (No Powerplant No. 2 IEVC conducted.)
8 May 88	23553	No. 2 Powerplant removed (to expedite change of Fuel Control Unit due overhaul) and refitted. (No Powerplant No. 2 IEVC conducted.)
4 Jul 88	23745	Last Scheduled P1 Maintenance Check conducted.
8 Jul 88	23764	Modification C061/61B35-64, improvements to MGB torquemeter cover oil passages, incorporated on No. 2 Torquemeter (MGB not removed).
13 July 88	23778	Accident.

*TSN - Time Since New in operating hours

1.6.4.3   No. 2 powerplant and drive train

The power turbine module of the No 2 Engine (SN 295223) was last overhauled during the 2nd Light Overhaul of the engine, which involved the almost complete stripping of the module. Amongst other actions carried out, bearings 4 and 5 were inspected and the PT oil jets were flow checked. The PT rotor, followed by the complete engine, were dynamically balanced on ground test rigs. A PT vibration level of 0 mils for the reassembled engine was achieved. Records for other engines which had passed through the same overhaul facility indicated that this was not abnormal.

The No 2 IDS and Thomas flexible coupling were last overhauled 2043 hours before the accident. The assembly was dynamically balanced at that time.

An IEVC was last conducted on ID's No 2 Powerplant following its installation in Oct 1987. Since then, it had been removed twice for maintenance actions and refitted, and the MGB had also been removed and refitted twice.

The MGB was last inspected at its Mid-Point Inspection in April 1988. Actions taken at this time included the standard replacement of both input free-wheel units with overhauled units.

There was no evidence of any abnormal failures or deficiencies having been found during the above overhauls and inspections. There was no evidence found of any anomalies in the inspection, repair and testing of components, or in the rebuild and testing of the engine, drive shaft or MGB, with the exception of that associated with the fitment of the polygon coupling (Para 1.12.3).

No abnormalities were found associated with the results of the last maintenance check, which was carried out 9 days/33 flying hours before the accident. No debris was found when engine No 2 MCDs were checked at this time.

1.7   Meteorological information

An aftercast of the weather for the area at the time of ditching was prepared by the Meteorological Office, Bracknell, and gave the following information:-

Synoptic situation - Complex low covered the United Kingdom with a moist easterly airflow around the Shetland Islands.

Weather: continuous light rain

Visibility: 5 - 8 km

Cloud:		1-3 oktas stratus, base 300 feet
		5-7 oktas stratus, base 6-800 feet
		8 oktas stratocumulus, base 1500 feet
		isolated imbedded cumulus, base 1000 feet, tops 7000 feet
Winds:	surface	090/10 kt
	2000 feet	110/12 kt
Sea water temperature:		13-14°(mean over five days)
Wave conditions.	wind wave:	0.5-1 metre, period 3-4 seconds
	swell wave:	0.5-1 metre, period 7 seconds
	significant wave:	1 metre every 4 seconds
	maximum wave:	up to 2.2 metres

1.8 Aids to navigation

The aircraft was equipped for Instrument Flight Rules (IFR) operations within the North Sea area.

1.9 Communications

On passing the Juliet reporting point at 1423 hrs, ID contacted Sumburgh Approach on 123.15 Mhz and remained on that frequency until it ditched. Only the Mayday call, and a second call about one minute later which referred to the fire on both engines, were heard by Sumburgh Approach. The final "ditching" call from ID was only heard by helicopter FK, which was being radar vectored to the last known position. The Sumburgh SAR aircraft joined the frequency at 1442 hrs, and the Cormorant SAR aircraft at 1519 hrs.

1.10 Aerodrome and approved facilities

Not relevant.

1.11 Flight recorders

No Flight Data Recorder (FDR) was required and none was fitted. A Fairchild A100 four track Cockpit Voice Recorder (CVR) of the endless loop type with a recording duration of 30 minutes was fitted, with recording tracks allocated as follows:

Track 1	Commander's microphone and headset signals.
Track 2	Main rotor rpm.
Track 3	Cockpit area microphone.
Track 4	Co-pilot's microphone and headset signals.

The CVR was installed in the rear fuselage. It was recovered undamaged, apart from the effects of seawater immersion, and a satisfactory replay was obtained by the AAIB Flight Recorder Section. Spectral analysis of the recording showed a change in the recorded signature over a period which terminated in an unusual noise (referred to as the "bang"). This was identified as that heard and remarked upon by the co-pilot, shortly before the No. 2 engine fire warning occurred. The signature change was manifest as a change in the amplitude of the signal, at a number of different frequencies:

TIME TO BANG min:sec	SIGNAL FREQUENCY Hz	EVENT
15:00	1970	First detected. Subsequently varied between 1970-1910 Hz with other transmission frequencies constant.
15:00	2380	First detected. Subsequently varied between 2380-2340 Hz with other transmission frequencies constant.
6:20	313	First detected, plus its harmonics. Subsequent steady signal strength increase.
5:30	2190	First detected. Frequency contant until bang.
2:20	626	Increase in signal strength (2nd harmonic of 313 Hz).
0:45		313 Hz sidebands on 1970-1910 Hz signal first detected.
0:10	313	Sudden marked increase in amplitude.
0:03	Nr	Nr, previously constant at 99.0%, began to decrease.
0:01	Nr	Nr, at 98.8% (-0.2%), began sharper decrease rate.
0	-	BANG
	313	Signal diminished in strength but remained detectable.
	1970	Disappeared.
	2380	Disappeared.
-0:01	Nr	Nr decreased to minimum of 96.0% (-3.0%).
-0:02	Nr	Nr increased to maximum of 99.4% (+0.4%).
-0:05	Nr	Nr stabilised at 98.9% (-0.1%).
-0:32		All frequencies began rapid decrease.

Normal frequencies of possible relevance, at 99% Nr, were:

313 Hz	-	Power turbine, IDS and input pinion 1/rev
118 Hz		Engine No. 5 bearing cage 1/rev
2145 Hz	-	Engine No. 5 bearing inner ring ball passing frequency
1298 Hz	-	Engine No. 5 bearing outer ring ball passing frequency

Analysis of CVR recordings from other S-61N helicopters showed that the PT/IDS/input pinion once/rev frequency was commonly present at high amplitude.

1.12 Examination of wreckage

1.12.1 Recovery

Following the accident, AAIB commenced a recovery operation using the Stena Marianos, a 99 metre long diving support vessel (DSV) with a dynamic positioning (DP) capability and provided with a saturation diving system capable of maintaining one diver on the seabed continuously. The ship was fitted with a small remotely operated vehicle (ROV) which could provide colour television pictures of the seabed within the range of its tether; with 2 Dukane acoustic beacon detector systems; and with a basic sidescan sonar system. Navigational information for the search was provided by a trisponder microwave ranging system. This was set up on the shores of the Shetland Islands and was potentially capable of indicating positions in the area of the site to within ±4 metres.

The Marianos arrived on site 7 nm east of Lerwick, Shetland Is, based on a Decca position supplied by the Lerwick Lifeboat crew, at 1800 hrs on 16 July 1988. At this position signals from the Dukane acoustic beacon fitted to the CVR were detected by hand-held Dukane detector equipment, deployed from an inflatable dingy. The beacon enabled rapid location of the aft fuselage section which, with the CVR still installed, was landed on deck at 0030 hrs on 17 July. Visual searching by diver and ROV of the seabed, in an area based on tide and wind drift predictions, located the forward fuselage section 500 metres from the aft fuselage section. This was recovered, together with a considerable number of items of scattered wreckage found. However, this first phase of the recovery operation had to be terminated at 2200 hrs on 19 July, because of other Marianos commitments, without the engines, the main rotor or the majority of the main transmission components having been found.

Shell Expro Ltd, ID's charterer at the time of the accident, offered facilities for the

2nd phase of the recovery operation. This commenced on site at 0200 hrs on 2 August 1988 using the Norskald, a 102 metre long DSV with a DP capability and equipped with a saturation diving system. This vessel was fitted with a small tethered ROV capable of providing monochrome silicon intensified target (SIT) television pictures of the seabed; and with a seabed-based, 100 metre range scanning sonar system. A trisponder system was again used for on-site navigation. The recovery operation was slowed by navigational difficulties, but the engines, the majority of the main transmission components and the main rotor were located at 0400 hrs on 5 August 1988 and raised the same morning.

1.12.2 *General*

The wreckage recovered in the 2 phases comprised virtually all parts of the aircraft that had survived the fire, with the exception of the right sponson, for which no recovery attempts were made. The engines were generally intact and still mounted in the remains of the engine bay structure. No parts of the magnesium alloy MGB casing or rotor brake housing were found, but all major components of the main transmission geartrain were recovered. The main rotor was substantially complete, although one blade was severely fire damaged.

Initial examination at sea of the recovered wreckage revealed that severe damage had been sustained by the structure and shafting connecting the No 2 engine to the MGB. The wreckage was transported to the AAIB at RAE Farnborough for more detailed examination.

1.12.3 **No 2 engine**

No 2 engine was generally intact. Strip inspection found no evidence of pre-shutdown failure or malfunction of the gas generator, but revealed severe damage to the PT No. 5 bearing and carbon rubbing seal. It was also found that extensive rotational rubbing of various parts of the PT rotor assembly against static parts of the module had occurred.

The PT wheel and turbine blades were intact, but the blade tips had been heavily rubbed by contact with the casing, over an arc consisting of approximately half the circumference. The aft faces of the remainder of the blade roots, and associated fasteners and dampers, had been heavily rubbed by contact with the forward static air baffle. No. 4 bearing, the worm gear and right angle drive, the spacer and the PT shaft all had an appearance suggestive of having been subject to overtemperature, but showed no gross indications of running damage.

The No. 5 bearing cage was recovered from the PT bearing housing in 19 main fragments. 8 of these were relatively undistorted and by fracture-matching could be assembled into an almost complete ring, which constituted half of the cage. It was apparent that the cage had split through the pocket webs on a central plane normal to the PT axis, and also fractured on a radial plane through the rail at the centre of most of the ball pockets. These pieces showed little sign of overheating affects and had generally retained their silver plating, which has a melting point of approximately 961°C. Most fracture surfaces were too severely damaged to show evidence of the fracture mode, but in one area, where a pocket side had cracked but had not completely fractured, clear evidence of fatigue was found by metallurgical examination. A number of the cage pieces also exhibited a second shiny band on the surface of the pocket, parallel and similar to the normal ball contact band, but nearer to the bearing centre. The other cage pieces were grossly distorted, consistent with having passed through No. 5 bearing while it was rotating. Metallurgical examination did not indicate that the cage had been subject to excessive temperatures.

The outer ring of No. 5 bearing was intact and free of gross wear or distortion, but had a small ridge on the aft shoulder adjacent to the trackway and a general appearance suggestive of overtemperature. The inner ring featured a grossly distorted and eccentric trackway, to the point where on one side it had thinned from a normal radial dimension of 0.17 inches, at the ring split plane, to almost nothing, and showed evidence of molten flow in some areas of the trackway and shoulders. The balls were all intact, with no signs of having skidded abnormally. Their diameter had been reduced by approximately 0.005 inches in all cases and, whilst remaining generally round, 4 balls positioned sequentially in the bearing exhibited a flattened or slightly concave equatorial band, consistent with their having run for a period in contact with each other.

Examination of ball and outer ring trackway surfaces revealed no signs of spalling. The inner ring trackway was too grossly damaged for meaningful evaluation, but close inspection of oil filter debris found a complete lack of typical spalling flakes. The material composition of all the components of the bearing was established using an electron microprobe analyser and found to be consistent with the required material specifications. Microsection examination revealed a white layer on the trackway surface of the inner ring which was confirmed to be carbide precipitation, in the form of a layer of untempered hard martensite. Rockwell hardness measurements on samples of the components gave values of 47-52 HRc for the outer ring, 45 HRc for a ball and 50-56 HRc for the inner ring, compared to the normal range for the modified 52100 steel of 58-62 HRc. The hardness/temperature relationship for this material was established by heating samples for 30 minutes at 100°C temperature increments and showed a softening to around 23 HRc at 750-800°C, and a rehardening above this temperature, to 49 HRc at 1000°C. This, together with the microsection evidence, indicated that the temperatures experienced had been in the order of 500-550°C for the outer ring, 600°C for the balls, and 1000°C for the inner ring.

Most of the PT carbon rubbing seal had been destroyed, with only a heavily rubbed portion of the carrier remaining. The seal mating ring was intact, but had eccentric heavy rubbing damage to its rim from contact with the rear seal housing, and a series of radial cracks on the surface of its forward face. The cracks contained a metallic deposit, which electron microprobe analysis showed to be silver, with some copper. A hardness survey across a section of the ring showed little direct evidence of overheating, and metallurgical examination concluded that the ring had been embrittled and cracked by a liquid metal penetration mechanism, associated with molten high temperature fragments of the silicon-bronze cage.

The polygon coupling was found, retained in-situ on the PT shaft by the shaft nut, with its '0' index mark displaced 120° from the shaft '0' index mark, and had clearly last been fitted in this position. Its forward collar section had suffered heavy rubbing on one side from contact with the bore of the rear seal housing. Checks showed specified hardness values (33-43 HRc) for the aft face but a marked softening of the forward face to 28 HRc, indicative of overtemperature. One corner of the triangular adapter had a heavy concave rub from contact with the bead of the EMRSA tube forward circumferential weld. Hardness measurement on the adapter gave no indication of overtemperature.

The engine oil system pressure filter element was found to be heavily loaded with small particles of metallic debris, identified as generally consistent with the bronze and steel components of No. 5 bearing. The oil pump had also been contaminated with metallic particles, and an elastomeric pump shaft seal showed signs of having been overheated. The seal condition was not consistent with the effects of an external fire, but appeared indicative of the pump having run briefly with an inadequate oil supply.

1.12.4 No 2 drive train

All Thomas coupling/adapter/IDS bolts and hi-loc nuts were in place. The Thomas coupling leaves were somewhat distorted and were severed radially next to one attachment bolt, consistent with bending overload due to excessive angular strain between PT and IDS axes, under static conditions. Additionally, an arc of the outer circumference of the leaves, together with the washers on one bolt, in the same circumferential location as the rubbed adapter corner, had been heavily rubbed by contact with the interior of the EMRSA. Thomas coupling/adapter bolt tails and nuts had also experienced severe angled rubs on their outboard corners, consistent with rotating contact with the belled forward end of the separated portion of the EMRSA (see below). The IDS was bent, again consistent with a static angular strain between PT and IDS axes, and in the same radial direction as the Thomas coupling. The IDS also exhibited a 6 inch longitudinal crack in the wall of its aft portion. Fracture surface examination revealed an intergranular appearance, suggestive of failure after the steel had been weakened at high temperature. A series of hardness measurements along the shaft showed an abrupt increase from 27 HRc forward of the canted firewall position (specified 26-33 HRc) to around 60 HRc aft of this, indicative of the shaft portion aft of the canted firewall having reached 900°C, or higher.

All 4 IDS T bolts and nuts were in position and the splined coupling was intact. Although sooted and with an appearance of having been subjected to overtemperature, this region was otherwise undamaged.

The EMRSA tube was severed circumferentially at the Thomas coupling axial station, immediately aft of the EMRSA forward circumferential weld, and heavy scrape marks on the internal surface of the tube adjacent to this failure could be matched to the adapter, Thomas coupling leaves and washers. The forward end of the separated portion of the EMRSA was petalled and belled, particularly downwards, with internal scraping that was consistent with rotational contact with the Thomas coupling bolt tails and nuts. The aft end of the EMRSA showed significant high temperature oxidation, suggestive of a temperature in excess of 1000°C.

1.12.5 Main gearbox bay

Virtually all of the MGB bay structure had been destroyed by the fire, except for the engine aft cowls and the canted firewalls. No parts of the magnesium alloy MGB casing were recovered, and no trace of the two magnesium alloy EMRSA/MGB aft isolators was found, although both of the mating steel yokes were recovered. Examination of the geartrain components, which included strip inspection of both input freewheel units, revealed no evidence of pre-ditching abnormalities. In particular, the No 2 input pinion showed no sign of running damage but had indications of severe overtemperature, with heat blackening and cracking of the forward journal surface. In addition, the associated white metal lining from both bearing cups had largely disappeared, with extensive rivulets of the alloy solidified on the cup flanges, indicating that it had melted and run out. Neither the spur gear journals nor the bearing cups showed any signs of rotational damage.

No part of the rotor brake housing was recovered, but most of the steel parts of the rotor brake were found including the disc, still attached to its shaft, and three pucks. The components showed no signs of pre-ditching abnormalities, and in particular there was no evidence of abnormal wear or extreme overheat to suggest that the brake had "dragged". The MGB oil pressure external pipeline routed close to the rotor brake disc (Para 1.6.2.4) was recovered and showed no evidence of contact with the rotating disc.

Inspection of all three generators showed no evidence of pre-ditching abnormalities.
No trace was found of the fuel or oil PXs, or the oil pressure switches, and the associated hoses could not be identified. All recovered hose remains that could possibly have formed part of these systems were examined, with no evidence of pre-ditching failure found.

1.12.6 Lifehatch

The lifehatch was intact and undamaged by fire, with latches fully withdrawn. Strip examination showed that the electrical actuator was in the fully retracted (*ie* lifehatch latched) condition. No evidence of deficiencies in the electrical or mechanical parts of the unlatching system on the lifehatch were found, but none of the airframe portion of the electrical system was available for examination.

1.12.7 ADELT

The remains of the ADELT, which was severely fire damaged, were found in the ADELT housing. Examination showed that the deployment cartridge had not fired, but under test it operated at an electrical current that was within limits.

1.13 Medical and pathological information

Not applicable.

1.14 Fire

The initial No 2 engine fire warning, 6 seconds after the bang, was followed after 1 min 40 secs by a No 1 engine fire warning, and a fire was corroborated after 2 mins 20 secs by the co-pilot's sighting of trailing smoke. Datumed on the bang, witness evidence indicated that wispy grey smoke started to enter the passenger cabin at 1½ - 2½ minutes, that this became acrid and then blacker at 3½ - 6½ minutes. Small flames were visible in the area around the No 2 engine exhaust at 6 minutes, and were quickly followed by growing signs of fire in the right side of the MGB housing. All of the witness evidence indicated that the fire was initially centred in an area close to the canted firewalls. Some 5 - 9 minutes after the ditching, FK's crew saw the blue paint above the rotor brake area turn to a greyish white, with flames around the main rotor mast but no signs of fire in the engine bay areas. The fire was described as spreading forwards and rearwards through the engine and MGB bays, before entering the cabin and progressively destroying the fuselage structure above the floor line.

The evidence from the wreckage as to the source and progression of the fire was limited because of the extensive destruction it caused, including loss of virtually all of the MGB bay structure, except for the engine aft cowls and the canted firewalls. A marked difference in the appearance of the internal surface of both aft cowls was apparent, with appreciably greater sooting aft of the canted firewalls than forward. Both canted firewalls showed signs of fire exposure, but evidence of material loss associated with hot fracturing along the bottom of the right hand firewall indicated that the fire had been hotter in this area than on the left side. Detailed examination of powerplant and MGB components (Para 1.12) indicated that the fire had been hotter in the forward part of the MGB bay than in engine bays.

1.15 Survival aspects

1.15.1 Flotation equipment

The only references to the flotation equipment in the operator's S-61N Operations Manual were the Arm and Inflate actions specified in the Ditching/Forced Landing Drill. These constituted: "Flotation Arming Switch......Armed" and "Inflate Switch--------Inflate". The Manual contained no descriptive or explanatory material on the flotation equipment, which it did for virtually all other aircraft equipment.

1.15.2 Evacuation management

The crew's actions during the evacuation were not in accordance with the Evacuation On Water Drill, which required, *inter alia* (C - Commander, P2 - Co-Pilot):
AFTER DITCHING
P2   Shut Down Engines ------ ------Rotor Coastdown
C   Embark Passengers in Aft Liferaft

In the event, the commander instead of the co-pilot had shutdown the No 1 engine and applied the rotor brake. The co-pilot, after donning his immersion suit, opened the forward (right) door and deployed the forward liferaft.

1.15.3 Lifehatch

The co-pilot believed that he had operated the lifehatch switches in the cockpit, but was unable to be certain. The required action was specified in the Evacuation On Water Drill as "P2 Dinghy Release Switch..............Operate". However, the cockpit switch, circuit breaker and warning light caption referred to "Emergency Door Jettison". It was noted that an assortment of terminology was employed in the Operations Manual to describe this item, including "Lifehatch", "Jettisonable Liferaft (Port Rear Emergency Door)", "Emergency Door" and "liferaft door". At no point did the Ditching/Forced Landing or Evacuation On Water Drills specify operation of the lifehatch Arm Switch.

It was also noted that the lifehatch description was contained in Section 3, Emergency/Abnormal Procedures, of the Operations Manual (Rev. 1 Dec 1986), rather than in Section 6, Systems Description, as for virtually all other aircraft equipment. Inspection of the operator's S-61N simulator after the accident revealed that the cockpit control panel for the lifehatch was not fitted, but at the time ditching and evacuation training was carried out in an aircraft rather than in the simulator.

The company which had chartered ID required all regular North Sea helicopter passengers to carry out comprehensive survival training, including experience of a 'dunker', such as that at The Robert Gordon Institute of Technology, Aberdeen. Immediately before their outbound flight to the rig, the passengers had been video-briefed in the departure lounge on S-61N ditching and evacuation procedures, including operation of the lifehatch. The exact difficulty experienced by the six passengers in the rear of the cabin in jettisoning the lifehatch was not identified, but the evidence indicated that it concerned the unlatching of the lifehatch, rather than its removal from the aperture after unlatching. No deficiencies in the placarded manual operating instructions on other aircraft in the operator's fleet were found, but it was noted that the passengers reported that their attempts to jettison the lifehatch took place in conditions of rapidly thickening noxious smoke.

1.15.4 ADELT

The ADELT did not deploy and the crew reported that they had not operated the Deploy Switch. The operator's Operations Manual contained a description of the ADELT, which stated that in the event of a controlled ditching a manual release of the ADELT would be carried out, but there was no reference to this in the Emergency Drills in the Operations Manual or the Emergency/Abnormal

Checklist.

1.16 Tests and research

1.16.1 Engine No. 5 bearing

Bearing No. 5 of the CT58-140 was intended to react predominately rearward axial loads of approximately 300 - 400 lb. While an axial load on this type of bearing produces similar contact angles with the inner and outer ring for each ball, a radial load causes variation in the angle as a ball orbits, and hence variation in the radius of the portion of the ring on which it runs and a consequent variation in the non-skidding rolling speed of each ball around the orbit. As balls are constrained by the cage to run at the same speed, such a radial load induces increased cyclic loads on the cage. The engine manufacturer has estimated that a radial load of the same order as the axial load, or larger, would be likely to cause serious cage distress.

Available information did not indicate that No. 5 bearing failure was common, but it did not prove possible to obtain quantitative data on service history. The engine manufacturer's Parts Support Digest T540 of 25 April 1986 noted the introduction of an improved No. 5 bearing (PN 50-1 3T34P01), with a steel cage and M50 steel for the other components, to be supplied when the inventory of the old bearing (PN 4003T47P01) was depleted and to be incorporated in engines on an attrition basis. In fact, the document was in error and the cage of the improved bearing was not changed to steel.

In April 1987 the engine manufacturer reported that operators had found very fine metal chips in new No 5 bearings of a different PN and recommended that, in the event of any such contamination being found, the bearing should either be returned for replacement or flushed and inspected before use. Additional manufacturing controls were introduced and no further field action was reportedly needed.

In February 1989 the engine manufacturer issued Overhaul Engineering Instruction (OEI) CT58-105 authorising: 'because of a critical fleetwide shortage of No 5 bearings and the excellent reliability of this part in service, the temporary extension of the service life of No 5 bearings inspected at overhaul and found satisfactory'. This was conditional upon an additional light overhaul of these bearings. The OEI anticipated that it would be cancelled in September 1989.

1.16.2 Clearance between Thomas coupling and EMRSA

The minimum clearance between the Thomas coupling and the EMRSA, with tolerances, was 0.131 - 0.150 inches. This clearance was between the coupling conical washers and the EMRSA tube internal surface, where contact would initially occur in the event of coupling radial excursion. Based on nominal dimensions, the excursion required to completely cut the tube would be the combination of this clearance and the 0.08 inch tube thickness, *ie* 0.211 - 0.230 inches.

The combined effects of the 0.005 inch undersize found in the No. 5 bearing balls and the 0.17 inch deformation of the bearing's inner ring trackway represented a No. 5 bearing play of 0.175 inches, in one radial direction. This corresponded, with the PT rotor constrained at the No. 4 bearing position, to about 0.25 inches radially at the position of the Thomas coupling.

1.16.3   IDS tests

During the investigation, tests were conducted to explore the possible effects of abuse of the Thomas coupling upon the dynamic balance of the IDS/Thomas coupling/adapter assembly. The first tests were carried out under AAIB control by a UK company approved for the overhaul of the S-61N IDS, using a scrap IDS on a 1000 rpm Shenck soft-bed dynamic balancing machine. Measurements were made of the incremental imbalance resultant from axial, torsional and bending loads which had been applied statically to the shaft assembly.

The effects found were minor, except in the case of a bending load that simulated the aft end of the IDS having been displaced radially until stopped by contact with the internal diameter of the EMRSA, with the adapter held rigidly. This involved a radial displacement of 1.3 inches, requiring a force of 44 - 54 lb. This case was intended to reproduce the maximum angular deformation that could be experienced by the Thomas coupling with the IDS and EMRSA remaining attached to an engine, such as could occur during engine removal from an aircraft, for example, where the engine was displaced relative to the MGB, with the IDS still engaged with the splined coupling. A balance change at the forward end of the assembly of up to 8.5 gm (at the balancing diameter of 2.69 inches) was measured, equivalent to a radial force of 257 lb at the nominal 100% speed of 18966 rpm.

The test was repeated under AAIB control and in conjunction with the aircraft manufacturer, by a USA company approved for the overhaul of the S-61N IDS, using the same scrap IDS, with a Hines hard-bed dynamic balancing machine running at between 500-1750 rpm. The test showed only a minor change in balance after a bending displacement of 1.3 inches, and did not repeat the results of the first test series. A different design of mandril and a different balancing machine were used for the two tests, but the reason for the difference in results was not established.

1.16.4　Previous cases

The S-61 type has been in extensive service since 1961 in many countries and many different civil and military versions. A considerable number of previous cases of fire were found recorded. However, the available details on most of the 69 cases examined were sparse, and an assessment of the relevance of a number of these cases to this accident was precluded by lack of information. Those known cases that did appear to be related, or at least exhibited similar features, were as follows:

1)　　Aircraft Type, SN and Accident Date - SH-3A, 61044, 22 May 1962

Whilst in flight the No 2 engine fire warning lights illuminated, followed by the muffled sound of an explosion and loss of No 2 engine torque. After carrying out the Engine Fire in Flight Drill and firing both extinguishers, the No 1 engine fire warning illuminated. Rotor speed decayed and the aircraft impacted onto water.

2)　　Aircraft Type, and Incident Date - H-62, Nov 1969

The aircraft concerned was a single-engined H-62 but the power train and engine rear support arrangement were reportedly similar to the S-61. The EMRSA was severed by the Thomas coupling. Relevant parts were not recovered and no further details were available.

3)　　Aircraft Type, Registration and Incident Date: S-61N, G-AZRF, 15 Sept 1976
　　　Engine SN　　　　　　　　　　　　　　　　295045

The aircraft was on a ferry flight without passengers. No 2 engine was at reduced power after an engine torque split had been experienced and the No 2 engine oil pressure had dropped, but remained within limits. Some 20 minutes into the flight, there was a loud bang and the No 2 engine fire warning lights illuminated. The Engine Fire in Flight Drill was executed, the fire warning lights eventually extinguished, and the aircraft landed safely.

Reports showed almost identical damage in some areas to that on ID's No 2 engine and drive train, with the No. 5 bearing cage broken-up and the inner ring trackway grossly distorted in an eccentric manner and severely overheated. The PT carbon rubbing oil seal had been destroyed. Severe rubs had occurred between rotating and static parts of the PT module and drive train, resulting in EMRSA severance by the Thomas coupling. In addition, No. 4 bearing was extensively damaged, the right angle drive gears were destroyed, and the oil pump was choked and its shaft fractured.

The No. 5 bearing oil supply nozzle on this engine was in the form of a tube, quite different from the pedestal type of nozzle on ID's No 2 engine. The damage was attributed to detachment of this nozzle tube as a result of fatigue failure initiated by distortion of the tube during reassembly of the PT module in an incorrect manner. No positive evidence for this conclusion was apparent in the available reports, and it was not known to what extent the investigation had considered the possibility that the nozzle failure had in fact resulted from excessive vibration loading associated with a bearing failure from other causes.

4)   Aircraft Type, SN and Incident Date   -   HH3E, 69-5804, Oct 1985
           Engine SN   -   285033

The aircraft suffered an in-flight fire, but no details of the events could be obtained. Investigation reports showed that damage in certain areas was very similar to that of ID's No 2 engine and drive train, with signs of the No. 5 bearing cage having broken and ridden on the outer ring. The No. 5 bearing inner ring trackway had grossly distorted in an eccentric manner and was severely overheated. The PT carbon rubbing oil seal was destroyed. Severe rubbing had occurred between the Thomas coupling and the EMRSA, resulting in severance of the latter. In this case the right angle drive gears had also broken up, causing loss of the PT speed signal to the FCU, and the PT wheel had suffered an overspeed non-containment. In addition, the Thomas coupling leaves and the bolts joining the adapter, Thomas coupling and IDS had suffered overload fractures. The ears of the IDS forward flange had broken-off, in the case of the one recovered ear because of extensive multi-origin fatigue. A SOAP had shown elevated levels of iron, bronze and silver over the 9 hours leading up to the failure.

One report attributed the failure to No. 5 bearing damage which had been caused by imbalance resulting from incorrect Thomas coupling assembly, but the strength of the evidence for this was not clear from the available information.

5)   General

From assessment of the available information on the previous fire cases it was also noted that:

a)   In none of the reported cases had an investigation concluded that an engine bay or MGB bay fire had caused mechanical rotating damage similar in any way to that sustained by ID's PT and drive train.

b)   In none of the reported cases, where severe rotating damage to bearings or shafting in the PT/drive train had been a feature, were vibration reports by crew or passengers noted as having been a precursor of the problem.

c) Ignition on engine exhaust duct surfaces of hydraulic fluid released in the forward end of the MGB bay had occurred on a number of occasions. Although this was generally associated with blade fold hydraulic systems, which were not fitted to the S-61N, this illustrated that ignition of such fluid release could occur.

1.16.5 Rotor brake

As the evidence indicated that the aircraft fire was initially centred in the rotor brake area, in-service experience of UK operators with the S-61N rotor brake was assessed. This uncovered a number of problems, including excessive or uneven puck wear, loose or missing puck screws, loose caliper bolt nuts and insufficient puck clearance from the disc with the brake released. These deficiencies, which had apparently first arisen only shortly before ID's accident, all had possible potentially hazardous consequences, such as fluid release onto the brake; puck release and forced ejection; and brake dragging when supposedly released. Appendix 6 details the findings on such rotor brake problems.

1.16.6 Firewalls

During inspection of six S-61N helicopters in-service it was noted that, with the aft cowls open, appreciable gaps existed between the canted firewalls and the annular fireseals mounted on the EMRSA (Para 1.6.2.2). It was possible that such gaps were altered by canted firewall distortion when the aft cowls were closed, but no clear evidence for this was established.

1.16.7 Lifehatch

In view of the difficulties reported by the rear passengers in opening the lifehatch, a test was conducted on 15 July 1988 on another S-61N, G-BFFJ, which was selected at random. The lifehatch failed to unlatch when the flight deck Emergency Door Jettison Switch was operated. Investigation showed that the latches had withdrawn by approximately 40% of their engagement length, but that the actuator had stalled at this point. This was probably because fretting wear had occurred to the latches when in their normal position engaged with the door frame ferrules, and had created a slight notch in the latches. The latches were also somewhat corroded and the load required to draw the notched latch profiles fully through the ferrules had apparently exceeded the actuator's capability. However, the lifehatch was successfully unlatched manually, with a horizontal force on the handle of 6-8 lb. After refitment, it unlatched satisfactorily in some 2 secs. when the flight deck switch was operated. A fleet check revealed no other cases of lifehatch failure to unlatch when the flight deck switch was operated.

1.16.8 MGB oil pipeline

The clearance between the rotor disc and the pipe supplying oil to the No 2 torquemeter appeared marginal on some S-61N's inspected and an investigation into this aspect was undertaken before the pipe from ID had been recovered. Considerable variation in the clearance was found on the seven aircraft inspected, and on two of them was only 5 mm. Factors that could affect the clearance included the depth to which the unions were screwed into the covers, the orientation of the pipe relative to the unions and the axial position of the brake disc (shimmed for centralisation in the rotor brake housing). There was no requirement in maintenance documentation for the clearance to be checked, nor was this normal practice.

A Special Check of this clearance was carried out on S-61N helicopters on the British Register. No cases were found of the pipe having contacted the disc.

1.16.9 Fuel pressure transmitter hoses

During the investigation, the circumstances of an engine bay fire that occurred on a Norwegian S-61N on 19 October 1988 were considered, in order to assess if there were any similarities to ID. That fire was attributed to ignition, on engine hot surfaces, of fuel sprayed from a leaking fuel PX flexible hose in the MGB bay (para 1.6.2.4). Abrasion of the hose against the canted firewall had reportedly resulted in a hole in the firewall and a breach in the hose. Examination of another crashed S-61N under investigation by AAIB (G-BDII, AAIB Aircraft Accident Report 3/89) revealed severe abrasion of both fuel PX hoses against the edge of the triangular titanium stiffening plate. The outer steel braid of both hoses had been completely cut through and the abrasion had progressed deep into the internal elastomeric tube. Each hose had been clamped to its associated drain hose at a position about mid-way along its length, but had no intermediate fixing to the canted firewall or other structure. In response to an AAIB recommendation to the CAA, a Special Check for damage and adequate fixing of the hoses was carried out on S-61N helicopters on the British Register.

1.17 Additional information

1.17.1 Engine Fire in Flight Drill

The S-61N Engine Fire in Flight Drill differed from fixed-wing practice in that it required the engine to be idled for 30 seconds after a fire warning, before any other action was taken. This was because a significant percentage of S-61N in-flight fire warnings had been caused by engine hot gas leaks. It was also reported by a major North Sea S-61N operator that over a number of years a high percentage of fire warnings had been caused by malfunction of the warning system.

1.17.2 Flight crew immersion suits

For the type of overwater public transport operation in which ID was engaged, The Air Navigation Order (Articles 13 and 33A and Schedule 5) required crew members to wear immersion suits when the sea temperature was predicted to be less than 10°C. The temperature limit was understood to represent the cut-off point for survival without a suit for a period in which rescue could be expected. The policy of BIH was for crew members to wear suits only when the CAA regulations required them to do so. This was understood to be intended to balance possible additional hazard in an emergency against possible detraction from the crew's performance that could result from fatigue and discomfort caused by wearing suits in normal operations. Another major helicopter operator has, for several years, applied its own more stringent conditions for the wearing of immersion suits. This has had the effect of requiring its crews to wear immersion suits for the majority of public transport flights over the North Sea.

2. ANALYSIS

2.1 Conduct of the flight

The muffled crack or bang heard by the co-pilot was the initial indication of a problem apparent to the crew, shortly followed by the No. 2 engine firewarning. The crew noticed no abnormalities in other indications and may well have been undecided as to whether the firewarning was genuine, nuisance or false. Most in-service S-61N engine firewarnings have either been false, or have been caused by hot gas leaks, and in fact the Engine Fire in Flight Drill reflected this, requiring the engine to be idled for 30 seconds and only shutdown if the firewarning persisted. Nonetheless, the crew reacted by promptly commencing a precautionary descent, starting the fire drill, and transmitting a distress call. The error in the RT call in identifying the problem engine as No. 1 was quite immaterial and the Drill was correctly actioned on No. 2 engine.

The illumination of the No. 1 engine firewarning, while the drill for No. 2 engine was being completed, presented the crew with a highly abnormal situation, and some continuing doubt about the validity of both warnings was indicated by the RT call expressing the intention to continue to the coast. It is possible that the first definite confirmation of a fire, when the co-pilot put his head out of the window and saw smoke, could have been obtained slightly earlier, but this would not have been easy until the aircraft had been slowed. Although this did not lead to any delay in ditching, as the crew's preceding approach had ensured that the aircraft was well placed to deal with developments, earlier confirmation of a serious fire would have been readily obtainable had the aircraft been fitted with rear view mirrors. It has therefore been recommended that the CAA require, for UK registered public transport helicopters, the fitment of rear view mirrors to provide the flight deck crew with an external view of the aircraft, enabling them to assess the nature and extent of external damage and fires. The decision of the crew to ditch was correct.

The single-engine ditching, with passengers pre-briefed, was well executed and was assisted by the relatively calm sea.. Although the floats were inflated before touchdown, rather than afterwards as required by drills, the ditching was well controlled and the buoyancy bags were not damaged. Had the bags suffered damage, stability would probably not have been in question, given the sea state, but the reaction loads associated with rotor brake application could have been significant, had it functioned. No positive evidence was found to indicate why the drill was not followed. It would appear that in the midst of dealing with a critical and highly abnormal situation the crew took the intuitive action of improving the aircraft's flotation capability before touching down. A contributory factor may have been the lack of any material in the operator's S-61N Operations Manual describing the emergency flotation system or explaining its use and the dangers of pre-ditching deployment, unlike most other systems on the aircraft. It has therefore been recommended that the CAA require that descriptive and explanatory material on the S-61N emergency flotation gear and its use be included in the Operations Manual, and that crew members receive adequate training in usage of the system.

2.2 Evacuation

The evidence indicated that the post-ditching shutdown and evacuation were handled well, and had not been compromised by not having been carried out totally in accordance with the Evacuation On Water Drill. The evacuation situation was potentially very serious, given the growing fire and rapidly thickening noxious smoke.

The usage of the rotor brake was in accordance with the Operations Manual but, as it failed to work effectively, probably as a result of fire damage (para 2.4.2), the commander's order to evacuate was marginally delayed by having to wait for the main rotors to stop.

The crew members were not required by the regulations to wear their immersion suits on this flight since the sea temperature was above 10°C (Para 1.7.2). After the ditching the co-pilot was occupied for a short period in donning his suit. It appeared likely that in this case no delay in evacuating passengers resulted, since the occupants had to wait for the rotors to stop. However, in slightly different circumstances either a serious delay in evacuation could have occurred while crew suits were donned, or the crew could have been forced to abandon the aircraft without wearing suits. As it was, the commander did not don his suit. The crew were responsible for directing an evacuation and subsequent proceedings on, or in, the water and any hazard to them could have also represented a hazard to the passengers.

BIH's policy of specifying the wearing of suits in flight only when this was required by CAA regulations was apparently reasonable in attempting to balance any crew performance loss in normal operations caused by wearing suits, against the additional hazard in an emergency of not having suits already donned. However, there was an inconsistency between this policy and that of another major North Sea public transport helicopter operator. As the two operators operated similar types of aircraft over similar routes, it was difficult to understand how each of the two different policies could have been optimised from the safety viewpoint. It has therefore been recommended that CAA establish the parameters for crew immersion suit wearing that would optimise overall safety, and regulate crew suit wearing for oversea public transport by UK helicopters in accordance with these parameters.

The difficulties encountered in unlatching the lifehatch increased the danger to six passengers at the rear of the cabin. The availability of push-out windows as another means of egress greatly improved their situation, but had evacuation through these been necessary it probably would have been slow, given the likely difficulties in finding and operating them in poor visibility, and in climbing through wearing immersion suit and life-jacket.

The evidence clearly indicated that the lifehatch did not unlatch electrically. The reasons for this could not be positively established, as the co-pilot was unable to be certain that he had operated the lifehatch Arm and Jettison Switches and a thorough assessment of the serviceability of the system at the time was precluded by fire damage. However, several factors likely to increase the chances of omission of correct action by the crew were identified. These included the lack of an instruction in the Checklist to arm the system. It has therefore been recommended that the CAA require that S-61N Checklists include an instruction to arm the lifehatch unlatching circuit in a ditching or forced landing situation. Another factor was the irregular Operations Manual format, with the lifehatch description in a different section from that of almost all other aircraft equipment, which was considered to be an unnecessary complication. Additionally, the widely differing terminology used between the Operations Manual, the Checklists and the aircraft panel was considered undesirable. In particular, the nomenclature in the Checklist of 'Dinghy Release Switch' allowed the possibility of confusion in an emergency with forward liferaft deployment. It has therefore been recommended that the CAA require that Operations Manuals follow a constant and logical format, and that equipment terminology in Checklists and Manuals correspond to that on aircraft panels.

The failure of the lifehatch unlatching test on another aircraft (para 1.16.7), while not proven to be relevant to the difficulties experienced on ID, did indicate that an improvement was required. It has therefore been recommended that the CAA require measures to improve the scheduled checking of the S-61N flight deck actuated unlatching system for the lifehatch, including regular measurement of the peak load required for manual unlatching.

No positive explanation for the difficulty experienced by the six passengers at the rear of the cabin in manually unlatching the lifehatch could be found. The placard instructions on similar aircraft of the operators fleet were clear and, while smoke may have prevented them from being read in ID's case, the coverage of the procedure in the passenger briefing video appeared to be quite adequate.

Passenger alarm at the sudden ditching and thickening noxious smoke, followed by the lifehatch failing to jettison, possibly contributed to a general confusion that led to the difficulty. However, there would seem little doubt that the passengers' capabilities would have been greatly improved had they been able to escape the noxious effects of the smoke and combustion gases. Additionally, in such circumstances gaseous products from the combustion of fuel, oil or furnishings can rapidly reach incapacitating or life-threatening concentrations. It has therefore been recommended that the CAA consider a requirement for the passengers on UK public transport helicopters to be provided with respiratory and eye protection from the effects of smoke and combustion gases arising from an on-board fire.

The crew members' inability to reach and aid the six passengers in the rear of the cabin was due to the lack of crew smokehoods or oxygen equipment stowed on or near ID's flight deck, and some time was lost in searching for a smokehood, as some aircraft in the operator's fleet were so equipped. It has therefore been recommended that the CAA urgently consider a requirement for the flight crew of UK public transport helicopters to be provided with accessible means of respiratory and eye protection from the effects of smoke and combustion gases arising from an on-board fire, as for fixed-wing public transport aircraft (Joint Airworthiness Requirement (JAR) 25.1439).

The crew omission of ADELT manual deployment selection before leaving the aircraft was possibly related to a general climate of feeling that deployment would be automatic in case of a ditching, in line with the title of the equipment. In fact, in a gentle ditching where the frangible switches remained intact the ADELT would not automatically deploy unless the aircraft capsized or took on large quantities of water, sufficient to cover the immersion switch in the plinth, well above the cabin floor level. A major contributory factor may well also have been the lack of any mention of the ADELT in the emergency drills. Had ID's ditching circumstances been somewhat less favourable, the occupant's survival could have depended on the ADELT. It was considered unsatisfactory that, two years after its incorporation throughout the operator's fleet, a simple revision of a Checklist card had not been made. The CAA, in the course of their flight standards monitoring function, had drawn the operator's attention to this omission, but the operator had failed to take action to rectify this. It has therefore been recommended that the CAA require measures to ensure that drill Checklists reflect the modification standard of the aircraft to which they relate, particularly where possible safety-critical items are concerned.

In addition, it has been recommended that the CAA conduct a review of S-61N emergency procedures for crews to ensure that the procedure for deployment of the ADELT, by manual selections from the cockpit, are included in crew checklists and carried out in simulated training.

2.3 No. 2 powerplant power turbine and drive train

2.3.1 *Cause of power turbine and drive train damage*

It was apparent that the PT and drive train of No. 2 engine had suffered significant pre-shutdown damage. This consisted of severe damage to No. 5 bearing, extensive rubbing between rotating and static parts of the PT module, and severe rubbing of the Thomas coupling against the EMRSA, which had resulted in severance of the latter. The only consistent explanation for the rubbing damage was that it had resulted from a failure that had allowed excessive radial excursion of the rear end of the rotating PT rotor, with the forward end of the rotor correctly constrained by No. 4 bearing. The latter was indeed found to have no apparent running damage. It was therefore concluded that the cause of the PT, EMRSA and drive train distress was the No. 5 bearing failure.

The play generated in No. 5 bearing by the dimensional changes found in its trackways and balls corresponded, with No. 4 bearing intact, to a Thomas coupling radial excursion of 0.25 inch, which approximately equalled the value required for the Thomas coupling to contact and cut through the wall of the EMRSA tube. The momentary dip in Nr and in PT/drive train rotational speed, which started 3 seconds before the bang, was consistent with the weakened EMRSA beginning to deform just before severance, thereby applying a sudden heavy torsional rubbing drag to the adaptor/Thomas coupling of No. 2 engine.

The possibility that contact between the adaptor/Thomas coupling and the EMRSA had resulted from some failure in the attachment of the EMRSA to the MGB was dismissed, since this would be expected to have produced heavily biased rubbing on the EMRSA interior, which had not occurred. Three other cases of EMRSA failure in association with deterioration of No. 5 bearing were known to have occurred (Para 1.16.4), and it appeared that there were commonly no indications of the deterioration available to the ground or flight crew until the EMRSA was severed. Such a failure was a potentially serious hazard, by virtue of the imposition of all the loads normally reacted by the EMRSA onto 19000 rpm shafting which was not intended to take such loads. It has therefore been recommended that the CAA require, for UK registered public transport S-61N helicopters, that measures be taken to ensure that excessive deterioration of the No 5 bearing of the engine shall not result in failure of the engine mounting rear support assembly.

2.3.2   Cause of No. 5 bearing failure

The cause of the No. 5 bearing failure could not be established directly from the bearing component evidence because of the severe mechanical and overheat damage that had been experienced subsequent to the initial failure, and seawater corrosion effects that had been accelerated by the degreasing action of the fire. However, it was apparent that there had been no fracture of the balls or rings, no prolonged ball skidding, and no signs of spalling of running surfaces, and a number of features were found which indicated that the bearing failure had initiated with a cage problem. It was concluded that the relatively undamaged cage fragments were part of the forward half of the cage that had broken off and fallen directly into the bearing support housing, whilst the heavily deformed fragments were parts of the rear half that had been severely deformed in their passage through the rotating bearing. Although few conclusions could be reached about the rear half of the cage, the lack of overheating evidence on the forward half indicated that it had broken up and fallen away before the severe overtemperature experienced by the balls and rings had occurred. This suggested that failure of the oil supply had not been a primary cause of the bearing failure, and this conclusion was reinforced by the lack of any signs of extended oil starvation in the engine as a whole.

The secondary ball running witness marks evident on the cage pocket surfaces indicated that the bearing had run comparatively smoothly with the cage significantly 'out-of-round', which could only have occurred after an axial fracture in the cage. Additionally, the evidence found on four adjacent balls that they had run rubbing against each other suggested that the bearing had run for a period with the cage split open across a number of pocket centres, and/or with a portion of the cage detached.

The spectral analysis of the CVR recording revealed a 313 Hz signal, first detected 6.3 minutes before the bang, that corresponded with the once/rev speed of the PT and the power drive train. Although such a signal was commonly present at high amplitude on other S-61N recordings, it behaved abnormally in this case by progressively increasing in amplitude, accompanied in the later stages by an increase in the amplitude of its 2nd harmonic (626 Hz). These features clearly indicated a developing problem associated with the PT or its drive train.

In addition, a 1970 Hz signal that was first apparent 15 minutes before the bang was notable both for its initiation, at a detectable amplitude at this point, and for its subsequent frequency variation while other transmission frequencies remained constant. It did not correspond with any of the normal rotational frequencies in the engines, drive trains or transmission, but possibly represented the inner ring ball-passing frequency for No. 5 bearing, modified from its normal value of

2145 Hz because of alteration of the bearing cage rotational speed as a result of a deterioration of the bearing. A depressed and erratic ball passing frequency would be consistent with the behaviour of a bearing with a cage that had broken and was either binding on the inner ring, or being affected by ball-bunching and consequent partial skidding. The analysis concluded that this was the most probable source of the signal. The basic drive train frequency sidebands on the 1970-1910 Hz signal, apparent 45 seconds before the bang, were fully consistent with adancing deterioration of the bearing.

The 2380 Hz signal, also first detected 15 minutes before the bang, varied its frequency in a somewhat similar manner to the 1970 Hz signal, and appeared to be associated with it, but its source could not be determined. The 2190 Hz signal was probably the 6th harmonic of the basic drive train frequency, and was again indicative of a significant defect in the drive train at this point.

Thus the available evidence, in combination, indicated that the primary bearing failure had been in the cage. It probably initiated with an axial break, followed by progressive fracturing across the centres of the pockets and detachment of cage sections.

It was possible that, during the break-up, cage displacement from its normal running position had caused the forward half of the cage to intercept the oil jet spray into the bearing and deflect it away from the inner ring chamfer, upon which it normally impinged. This would have contributed to an initial temperature increase and deterioration of the rings and balls. The high degree of overtemperature experienced by the rings and balls was probably the result of the balls running in contact with each other, unseparated by the cage. A contributory factor was likely to have been a marked deterioration in oil capture by the bearing, as a result of the oil spray increasingly missing its inner ring chamfer target as the play in No. 5 bearing increased and the inner ring moved aft, under the influence of the PT rotor thrust load.

2.3.3 *Cause of No. 5 bearing cage failure*

The available evidence was not sufficient to positively establish the cause of the bearing cage failure. However it was established, with a reasonable degree of confidence, that the reliability of the bearing in this application was good, and that cage failure was not common.

Some evidence of cage fatigue cracking was found, but no positive conclusions as to its cause could be reached. The possibility that the cage was defective in some way could not be dismissed, although no indications of this were found. There was considerable evidence to support the alternative possible cause, namely that of bearing radial overload. The degree of eccentricity of all the mechanical damage to the rotating components (PT wheel and blades, No. 5 bearing inner ring, carbon rubbing seal mating ring, polygon coupling, adaptor and Thomas coupling) was most marked in comparison with the even circumferential rubbing of the corresponding static components. In addition, the relative directions of these eccentric rubs were all indicative of the effect of a radial force acting on the aft end of the PT rotor assembly, in a constant radial direction relative to the rotor.

The possibility that the eccentricity had been a result, rather than a cause, of No. 5 bearing failure was considered. A degree of bias of the wear could have been expected to result, if whirling of the PT/IDS combination had resulted from excessive play in No. 5 bearing. However, in the absence of a significant radial force on the PT/IDS, it was considered likely that such whirling would have precessed as resultant mechanical damage caused progressive alteration in the PT/IDS balance state, rather than acting in a constant radial direction throughout. Similarly, local off-centring of the PT/IDS axis as a result of No. 5 bearing ball-bunching following cage failure would not have acted in a constant direction on the rotor, given continued ball circulation, as was indicated by the lack of signs of prolonged ball skidding. Excessive radial loading on a bearing of this type has been known to result in cage failure and consequent deterioration of the other components of the bearing. It was therefore concluded that an excessive radial force, acting in a constant rotor radial direction on the aft end of the PT rotor, was the most likely cause of the No. 5 bearing failure, although the possibility that it had resulted from a cage defect could not be dismissed.

2.3.4   *Cause of No. 5 bearing overload*

The only sources of a rotating radial force that could be envisaged were either an imbalance at the aft end of the PT rotor, or a defect in the drive train which had caused a rotating bending moment to be applied to the IDS. Other possibilities, such as imbalance towards the front of the PT rotor or the rear of the drive train, would be expected to have had their predominant effect on No. 4 bearing or on the input pinion bearings respectively. Excessive offset or angular misalignment of the PT and MGB axes would have been expected to have caused eccentric damage to static parts and regular damage to rotating parts, rather than vice versa.

The misalignment of the polygon coupling and PT shaft index marks raised the possibility of an imbalance having resulted from fitment of the polygon coupling in an incorrect position with respect to the PT shaft, although it was also possible that this was simply a case of an indexing error. However, the satisfactory vibration levels obtained at the IEVC which was conducted after the installation of the powerplant in ID on 29 October 1987 showed that either incorrect fitment had not occurred at the 2nd Light Overhaul, or that incorrect fitment at this time had not significantly unbalanced the powerplant. The operator's records did not indicate that any work had been done on the powerplant subsequent to initial installation which would have required polygon coupling removal. Thus it was not possible to establish when the coupling had been incorrectly fitted or wrongly indexed. Incorrect fitment of the polygon coupling appeared unlikely to have been the cause of imbalance which led to No. 5 bearing failure, but could not be totally dismissed.

The IDS/splined coupling re-orientation procedure was questionable in implicitly utilising a change in balance at the rear of the IDS to effect a change in vibration at the front. This procedure appeared to have been employed because the action of re-orientation of the IDS forward joint, between adaptor and polygon coupling, was impossible with the engine in its powerplant configuration and the forward joint totally inaccessible inside the EMRSA. The technique apparently worked by generating an imbalance at the rear joint, that transferred excitations via the IDS and EMRSA in such a way as to partially nullify the vibrations sensed by the PT transducer from forward joint imbalance. It appeared that vibratory loading would not be reduced on No. 5 bearing by this method and would, in fact, be increased on the input pinion bearings. Although the evidence did not suggest that this was a factor in this accident, it has nevertheless been recommended that the CAA review the acceptability of the procedure whereby S-61N PT vibration levels are adjusted by re-orientation of the joint between IDS and splined coupling.

The lack of any rotational damage to either the input pinion bearings or journals, or to the splined coupling fall-back bearing, indicated that a failure in the input pinion area had not been a factor. No plausible explanation, consistent with the evidence, of how a fire in the MGB bay (Para 2.4) could have caused the failure of No. 5 bearing was found, and it was concluded that the fire had probably resulted from the bearing failure, rather than having been its cause. The possibility that a rotating radial force on No. 5 bearing had been generated by a defect that had locked the splined coupling and prevented it from providing its normal degree of angular flexibility could be dismissed since the coupling showed no signs of the mechanical distress that would have been expected in such a case.

However, the results of rig tests on a sample adapter/Thomas coupling/IDS assembly were significant in indicating that relatively minor mishandling could produce a permanent set in the coupling's leaves that manifested itself as a large imbalance at the forward end of the IDS assembly. This effect was not repeated during a second test using a different balancer and mandril but, as the reasons for this could not be established, it was unclear which of the two tests more closely simulated the aircraft situation. A practical means of measuring the effect on an aircraft of an IDS assembly mishandled in this way could not be found. No evidence was found of cases of such a problem being encountered in-service. However, available details on previous failure cases were generally very sparse and the possibility that such an effect had been encountered, but not identified, could not be dismissed. Thus, while the apparent lack of service experience made it unlikely, the possibility that accidental bending of the assembly could generate an imbalance force of the same order as that necessary to cause No. 5 bearing distress (para 1.16.1) could not be dismissed.

2.3.5 *The cause of Thomas coupling distortion*

The occurrence during in-service maintenance of the above type of mishandling, namely static radial displacement of the aft end of the IDS until it contacted the EMRSA (*ie* a displacement of 1.3 inches, requiring a force of 44 - 54 lb) could be envisaged in circumstances where the powerplant was separated from the MGB. In particular, there seemed to be a reasonable possibility that the problem could occur during removal or installation of the powerplant or MGB should either be moved relative to the other without the IDS being completely separated from its register with the splined coupling. Alternatively, such a displacement could occur from accidental contact with the IDS end, protruding beyond the EMRSA end, either on or off the aircraft. The displacement involved was relatively small, as was the force required to produce it, and there would be no compelling visual indication that it had occurred. No particular cautions against such an apparently minor abuse, or its possible effects, were found in the Aircraft or Engine Manuals.

Such a problem would be readily detected by the monitoring of PT vibration levels, but for G-BEID this had last been done 727 operating hours before the accident. In the intervening period No. 2 powerplant and the MGB had each been removed and refitted twice, ie four occasions on which the powerplant and MGB had been separated without a subsequent IEVC. Airframe vibration checks had been conducted during this period, but these measured levels in the cockpit and it was likely, given the vibration isolators incorporated in all three powerplant mounts, that such checks would not detect a localised imbalance in the No. 5 bearing area.

It was concluded that there had been the opportunity for accidental excessive bending of the Thomas coupling and that, if this had occurred, any resultant imbalance would not have been detected because an IEVC was not conducted following engine/MGB reconnection and no means of continuously monitoring vibration levels was provided.

2.3.6   Vibration monitoring

The lack of IEVC's was in accordance with the operator's normal procedures, but the aircraft manufacturer considered that, in the case of engine change situations, these did not match the AMM requirements. The situation may have arisen because of lack of definition in the supplementary instruction (SI) in the Manual as to whether "replaced" was intended to refer only to substitution of a different engine or also to reinstallation of an engine. This obvious ambiguity had apparently been addressed in a revision to part of the relevant chapter, issued a month after promulgation of the SI, that referred to "installation or reinstallation of an engine". However, ample scope for confusion still remained due to the SI's claim that "it was to take precedence where it is at variance with the manual". These ambiguities were obvious and it was surprising that they had apparently not been raised between the operator and manufacturer, and resolved.

The lack of a requirement for an IEVC following MGB substitution or reinstallation, and indeed a positive statement by the aircraft manufacturer in 1985 that it was not required, was illogical when it was known that changes at the joint between IDS and splined coupling could make a significant difference to PT vibration levels. Indeed, such reorientation of the IDS relative to the splined coupling was the specified procedure in the AMM for reducing PT vibration to acceptable levels. It has therefore been recommended that the CAA require an IEVC to be conducted before public transport flight following any disturbance of the S-61N IDS/splined coupling joint, and also require this to be clearly expressed in UK operators' Manuals.

The monitoring of PT vibration levels would undoubtedly be a reliable means of detecting such a problem as Thomas coupling distortion, but a continuous vibration monitoring facility was not provided for this or any other components on the S-61N, in common with most helicopters. Nor had it been the practice for a number of years to conduct the non-mandatory Aircraft Vibration Check contained in the AMM. This paucity of monitoring is surprising in view of the obvious importance of vibration as the primary reflection of the mechanical health of high speed rotating equipment. Much of such equipment on a helicopter is of vital importance. Indeed, it has been found in a number of cases where failure of such equipment has led to a serious accident that prolonged warning of the developing failure was provided by a change in vibration signature. This has been detected by the CVR, but has only been apparent on post-accident analysis, and/or has been evident to passengers.

It is recognised that work on helicopter condition monitoring improvements is in progress, but in-service provision of continuous vibration monitoring systems, which have been available for many years, is considered long overdue. It has therefore been recommended that CAA require, for all UK public transport helicopters, the early provision of a facility to continuously monitor the vibration of all high-speed rotating equipment whose integrity is critical to flight safety. A similar recommendation was made in AAIB Report 3/88, published in June 1988.

It has also been recommended that CAA require for all UK registered public transport helicopters without effective continuous vibration monitoring systems, vibration checks both on a routine basis and following disturbance of high-speed rotating equipment whose integrity is critical to flight safety.

2.3.7 *General health monitoring*

In addition to the lack of vibration monitoring, the other means of monitoring the mechanical health of the engines appeared limited. No form of oil analysis programme was specified for the engine oil system and there was no cockpit indication or warning of oil system contents, pressure filter blockage nor MCD condition. In fact, although MCDs were referred to as "chip detectors" in the engine manuals, the only indication of engine state provided by the MCDs was at the visual inspection scheduled at 50 hour intervals. The likely standard of interpretation of such indications was questionable, given the lack of a specified procedure for the action required when debris was found. It has therefore been recommended that CAA require that clear written instructions are provided to maintenance personnel on health monitoring systems whose effectiveness may have significant effects on flight safety. In addition, it has been recommended that the CAA require, for all public transport helicopters, the provision of cockpit indications of engine oil systems reservoir contents and chip-detector warnings.

No reason was found to doubt the general opinion of many professionally associated with the S-61N that its engine had demonstrated an excellent level of reliability in-service. Nonetheless, experience has shown that in the absence of comprehensive means of condition monitoring, a fault that develops on a gas-turbine can progress to an advanced stage without detection. It has therefore been recommended that CAA require, for UK public transport S-61N helicopters, a review of the standard of engine condition monitoring, and the improvements necessary to achieve an adequate level.

2.4 Fire

2.4.1 *Initiation of the fire*

Given the fine flatness tolerance of the PT carbon rubbing oil seal and mating ring, there was little doubt that engine oil would have have been released past it into the EMRSA at an early stage of the No. 5 bearing deterioration. Subsequent high-speed rubbing of the polygon coupling, adaptor and Thomas coupling against static components would have generated local hot spots, and metallurgical examination confirmed such effects. It was therefore concluded that the initial fire had probably resulted from ignition of engine oil within the EMRSA. It was also possible that, even without the rubs that had occurred in this case, oil leaking into the EMRSA could be ignited, as there was a natural sump area at the forward end of the EMRSA and experience had shown that oil tended to find its way through the unsealed EMRSA/PT casing joint and onto the exhaust casing. The latter had a normal operating temperature well above the oil's auto ignition temperature. It has therefore been recommended that the CAA require, for UK public transport S-61N helicopters, measures to drain the engine mounting rear assembly tube of any oil which leaks past the carbon rubbing oil seal located aft of the No 5 bearing.

The small clearance found to exist on S-61N aircraft between the No 2 torquemeter oil pipe and the rotor brake disc was a matter of concern, particularly as this pipe on ID had been disturbed 14 hours before the accident (para 1.6.4.2) and as the fire appeared to be centred in the same area. When the pipe from ID was recovered it was clear that it had not been in contact with the disc, and the Special Check showed no cases of this having occurred on other aircraft. However, the clearance appeared marginal and was not normally subject to any check. It has therefore been recommended that the CAA require, for UK public transport S-61N helicopters, measures to ensure adequate clearance between the No 2 torquemeter oil pressure pipe and the rotor brake disc, including associated amendment of the S-61N Maintenance Manual.

The possibility of fuel release from the fuel PXs or associated flexible hoses in the MGB bay was considered closely, particularly in view of the witness evidence which indicated that the fire was centred in the area where they were located. The investigation was hampered by a lack of any identifiable components from these systems but, when it became clear that the No 2 engine failure could not have been caused by a fire, it was possible to conclude that a failure in the fuel PX system had not been a primary cause of the fire. However, the severe PX hose abrasion damage found on a UK S-61N and reported on a Norwegian S-61N in the course of the investigation was of concern, particularly as the latter case demonstrated the potential for a fire to occur as a result. It has therefore been recommended that the CAA require additional inspection of the fuel pressure transmitter hoses on UK public transport S-61N helicopters, and alert the authorities of overseas S-61N operators to this problem.

In addition, it has been recommended that the CAA require, for UK public transport S-61N helicopters, measures to ensure that satisfactory separation of the fuel pressure transmitter hoses from adjacent structure and components is maintained.

2.4.2 *Progression of the fire*

The extensive destruction that resulted from the fire, together with the disruptive effects of the break-up and sinking of the aircraft remains, severely handicapped assessment of the progression of the fire. However, general visual inspection together with detailed metallurgical examination of components of the No. 2 powerplant and drive train showed that, apart from local hot spots, the aft portion of the drive train had experienced considerably higher temperatures than the forward end. A crack in the aft end of the IDS was characteristic of a high temperature failure, and metallurgical evidence indicated that the aft end of the IDS and EMRSA had experienced at least 900°C and 1000°C respectively, the temperature profile increasing sharply aft of a position roughly corresponding with the canted firewall. Thus it was apparent that the fire had been hotter in the MGB bay than in the engine bay, but the lack of any rotational damage to either the splined coupling fall-back bearing or to the input pinion bearings or journals, in spite of the severe overtemperature and mechanical damage to the latter, indicated that the severe overheat had only occurred after No 2 engine had been shutdown. The observations of FK's crew, at a time estimated at between 8-12 minutes after the bang, of discoloured paint above the rotor brake area and flames around the main rotor mast but no signs of fire elsewhere, including engine bay regions, was also consistent with the fire having been centred in the forward part of the MGB bay, in its intermediate stage.

Attempts to identify the major fuel source of the fire by chemical analysis of soot deposits were inconclusive. The consensus of the witness evidence that the initial smoke seen was generally grey and only became blacker when the fire entered the cabin 5-6 minutes after the bang, suggested that oil or hydraulic fluid were involved initially. Additionally, it was known from passenger witnesses that significant quantities of oil, which subsequent analysis identified as MGB oil, had been released some 90 seconds after the initial bang, and it was reasonable to suppose that this was ignited by a primary engine oil fire in the EMRSA. The available evidence indicated that the probable cause of this major oil release was damage to the MGB input oil seal, casing or oil lines, either as a result of overheat from the initial fire in the EMRSA, or due to excessive forces applied by the IDS following EMRSA severance. In the absence of any parts of the MGB casing, the exact reasons remained speculative.

Possible further flammable material sources in this region were:
(a) Engine oil that had been released because of a failure in the engine oil PX, pressure switch or associated pipelines.
(b) Hydraulic fluid released as a result of failure of the rotor brake or its supply lines.
(c) Kerosene released because of a failure of the fuel PX or associated pipelines.
(d) The magnesium alloy of the MGB casing.
The passengers' description of the smoke 3-4 minutes after the bang as acrid and bitter was possibly indicative of burning hydraulic fluid, and this could have been consistent with the rotor brake failure discovered when the attempt was made to apply it at around 4.5 minutes after the bang. The reason for the metal-metal noise coincident with brake lever application was not positively established, but the most likely reason in the circumstances for the lack of lever resistance, given the indications from the wreckage that the pucks had survived the fire, was overheat failure of piston/cylinder fluid seals.

2.4.3 *Firewalls*

The gaps between the canted firewall and the EMRSA annular fireseal, found to be common on S-61N aircraft inspected, could have been altered by firewall distortion caused by aft cowl closure, but it was not possible to establish whether the gaps were generally eliminated by this effect. Such gaps were of concern since, if they were present with aft cowls closed, they would constitute breaches in the firewalls separating the engines from the MGB bay. It has therefore been recommended that the CAA require a review of S-61N engine bay firewall integrity, to ensure that significant gaps in the fireseal arrangement at the points where the engine mounting rear support assembly tubes pass through the canted firewalls are eliminated when the aft cowls are closed.

The EMRSA effectively formed part of the firewall, and the 16 mm hole in the EMRSA wall, provided for Thomas coupling inspection (Para 1.6.2.2.), constituted a significant breach. It has therefore been recommended that the CAA require measures to improve S-61N engine bay firewall integrity by blanking the inspection hole in each engine mounting rear support assembly tube.

2.4.4 *Fire protection*

Although the evidence indicated that the root cause of the fire was an engine problem, the resultant fluid release and ignition occurred in the MGB bay. That the consequent uncontrollable fire could occur in such a gearbox bay is readily understood when the nature of the bay's contents are considered, namely extensive flammable fluid systems in proximity to high speed rotating equipment, with possible single-failure modes that would release fluid adjacent to areas of high temperature rubbing. This raised questions concerning the adequacy of the design and certification criteria whereby such a bay is not designated as a fire zone and is therefore not required to be thermally isolated from the remainder of the aircraft, or provided with fire detection and extinguishing capability, and flammable fluid shut-off systems.

In this case, the achievement of the ditching and evacuation in time for all of the occupants to escape appeared primarily due to the crew having been alerted to the presence of the uncontrollable MGB bay fire by the early operation of the fire detectors in both engine bays. However, the firewarnings appeared to have been a fortuitous accident of the firewire layout in the engine bays, rather than an intended design feature. It has therefore been recommended that the CAA review the fire protection provision needs of helicopter MGB bays, including the fitment of thermal isolation means, fire detection and extinguishing systems, and flammable fluid shut-off systems. A similar recommendation was made in AAIB Report 7/84, published in January 1985.

2.5 Rotor brake

The investigation indicated that the errors, changes and lack of identification on the brake units of incorporated modifications had led to puck screws of incorrect length being utilised on other S-61N brake units. It was also apparent that caliper bolt nuts on other units had probably been overtorqued during overhaul, due to contradictory torque values between the brake Overhaul Manual and the Aircraft Maintenance Manual, and that this had led to nuts becoming loose on their bolts. It has therefore been recommended that the CAA require that the S-61N rotor brake maintenance and overhaul documentation be thoroughly reviewed and errors and sources of confusion eliminated.

In addition, it was found that a design feature of the rotor brake torqueless grip modification could result in a condition, not apparent externally, in which the internal gap would be lost and the puck would ratchet towards the disc during initial brake applications, finishing up in contact with the disc when the brake was released. Although post-installation tests should reveal such a situation, the feature represented an unnecessary degradation in the potential safety of the system. In view of the severe potential consequences of a dragging rotor brake, it has been recommended that the CAA require that the design of the S-61N rotor brake torqueless grip modification be reviewed.

3. CONCLUSIONS

3a) Findings

1. The crew was properly licensed and medically fit to conduct the flight.

2. The helicopter had been maintained in accordance with an approved maintenance schedule, and the Certificates of Airworthiness and Maintenance Review were valid.

3. The aircraft caught fire while in the cruise, with no prewarning of a problem. The fire was initially centred in the forward part of the MGB bay.

4. The crew was alerted to a problem by the sound of a bang, rapidly followed by activation of both engine fire warnings, and smoke confirmed the presence of a fire. A gentle ditching onto the North Sea was achieved 3 minutes after the initial indications of a problem.

5. The emergency flotation bags were deployed before touchdown, in error, but were not damaged. Deficiencies in the Operations Manual may have contributed to the premature deployment.

6. Although all occupants evacuated the burning aircraft successfully into liferafts and were subsequently airlifted to safety uninjured, evacuation was hampered by noxious smoke in the cabin and by lack of smoke masks for passengers or crew. Such smoke protection was not required by Airworthiness Regulations for public transport helicopters.

7. The crew did not divide their post-ditching shutdown and evacuation duties completely in accordance with the drills. This did not compromise the evacuation.

8. Evacuation into liferafts was slowed by failure of the rotor brake to function, as a result of the fire.

9. Evacuation was hindered by failure of the lifehatch to unlatch electrically. The reasons for this could not be established, but Checklist and Operations Manual deficiencies that could contribute to omission of the selection were identified, and tests on other aircraft indicated a need for more frequent and comprehensive checking of the system.

10. The Automatically Deployable Emergency Location Transmitter did not deploy. Manual deployment selection by the crew was not required by drills, and conditions for automatic deployment were not met until after the ADELT had been disabled by fire damage.

11. The evidence indicated that the fire probably resulted from deterioration of the power turbine thrust bearing of the No 2 engine which caused engine oil to leak into the EMRSA tube and the drive train to rub and eventually sever the tube. The oil was probably ignited either by hot spots, resulting from the rubbing, or by the engine exhaust casing hot surface.

12. MGB oil was released as a result of damage caused either by the engine oil fire, or by the EMRSA severance, and probably ignited by the burning engine oil. Hydraulic fluid, kerosene and the magnesium alloy of the MGB contributed to the fire, which eventually consumed most of the aircraft above floor level.

13 There was no requirement or provision for fire detection, containment and/or suppression systems in the MGB bay, despite the extensive presence of flammable materials and potential ignition sources.

14. The No. 5 bearing deterioration resulted from failure of the bearing cage, caused either by a defect in the cage, or by excessive imbalance forces on the bearing. Possible causes of imbalance were incorrect fitment of the polygon coupling or distortion of the Thomas coupling due to mishandling, although no evidence was found that either had occurred.

15. No continuous means of detecting engine imbalance, such as a continuous vibration monitoring facility, were provided. No installed engine vibration check had been conducted following the last four connections of the No 2 engine with the MGB, because of deficiencies in the Maintenance Manual requirements.

16. Few other indications were available to crew or to maintenance personnel to enable the mechanical health of the engines to be monitored, and no pre-warning of the failure was received.

17. Spectral analysis of the CVR recording revealed abnormalities in the vibration signature from 15 minutes before the bang.

18. A number of other potential problem areas and deficiencies were identified that proved not to have a bearing on this accident but require action or review.

3b) **Cause**

The accident was caused by an uncontrollable fire in the main gearbox bay which probably resulted from the effects of failure of the No 5 bearing in the No 2 engine. An underlying factor was the lack of any fire detection or suppression capability within the main gearbox bay. The cause of the bearing failure could not be positively established.

4. **SAFETY RECOMMENDATIONS**

The following Safety Recommendations were made to the CAA during the course of the investigation: that the CAA:

4.1 Require, for UK registered public transport helicopters, the fitment of rear view mirrors to provide the flight deck crew with an external view of the aircraft, enabling them to assess the nature and extent of external damage and fires. (Made July 1990).

4.2 Require that descriptive and explanatory material on the S-61N emergency flotation gear and its use be included in the Operations Manual, and that crew members receive adequate training in usage of the system. (Made 21 November 1989).

4.3 Establish the parameters for crew immersion suit wearing that would optimise overall safety, and regulate crew suit wearing for oversea public transport by UK helicopters in accordance with these parameters. (Made 21 November 1989).

4.4 Require that S-61N Checklists include an instruction to arm the lifehatch unlatching circuit in a ditching or forced landing situation. (Made May 1990).

4.5 Require that Operations Manuals follow a constant and logical format, and that equipment terminology in Checklists and Manuals corresponds to that on aircraft panels. (Made 21 November 1989).

4.6 Require measures to improve the scheduled checking of the S-61N flight deck actuated unlatching system for the lifehatch, including regular measurement of the peak load required for manual unlatching. (Made 14 April 1989).

4.7 Consider a requirement for the passengers on UK public transport helicopters to be provided with respiratory and eye protection from the effects of smoke and combustion gases arising from an on-board fire. (Made 21 November 1989).

4.8 Consider a requirement for the flight crew of UK public transport helicopters to be provided with accessible means of respiratory and eye protection from the effects of smoke and combustion gases arising from an on-board fire. (Made 14 April 1989).

4.9 Require measures to ensure that drill Checklists reflect the modification standard of the aircraft to which they relate, particularly where possible safety-critical items are concerned. (Made 21 November 1989).

4.10   Conduct a review of S-61N emergency procedures for crews to ensure that the procedure for deployment of the ADELT, by manual selections from the cockpit, are included in crew checklists and carried out in simulated training. (Made 14 April 1989).

4.11   Require, for UK registered public transport S-61N helicopters, that measures be taken to ensure that excessive deterioration of the No. 5 bearing of the engine shall not result in failure of the engine mounting rear support assembly. (Made 14 April 1989).

4.12   Review the acceptability of the procedure whereby S-61N power turbine vibration levels are adjusted by re-orientation of the joint between the input drive shaft and the splined coupling. (Made 21 November 1989).

4.13   Require that an installed engine vibration check be conducted before public transport flight following any disturbance of the S-61N IDS/splined coupling joint, and also require this to be clearly expressed in UK operators' Manuals. (Made 14 April 1989).

4.14   Require, for all UK public transport helicopters, the early provision of a facility to continuously monitor the vibration of all high-speed rotating equipment whose integrity is critical to flight safety. (Made 21 November 1989).

4.15   Require, for all UK registered public transport helicopters without effective continuous vibration monitoring systems, vibration checks both on a routine basis and following disturbance of high-speed rotating equipment whose integrity is critical to flight safety. (Made July 1990).

4.16   Require that clear written instructions are provided to maintenance personnel on health monitoring systems whose effectiveness may have significant effects on flight safety. (Made 21 November 1989).

4.17   Require, for all public transport helicopters, the provision of cockpit indications of engine oil systems reservoir contents and chip-detector warnings. (Made 14 April 1989).

4.18   Require, for UK public transport S-61N helicopters, a review of the standard of engine condition monitoring, and the improvements necessary to achieve an adequate level. (Made 21 November 1989).

4.19   Require, for UK public transport S-61N helicopters, measures to drain the engine mounting rear assembly tube of any oil which leaks past the carbon rubbing oil seal located aft of the No. 5 bearing. (Made 14 April 1989).

4.20 Require, for UK public transport S-61N helicopters, measures to ensure adequate clearance between the No. 2 torquemeter oil pressure pipe and the rotor brake disc, including associated amendment of the S-61N Maintenance Manual. (Made 14 April 1989).

4.21 Require additional inspection of the fuel pressure transmitter hoses on UK public transport S-61N helicopters, and alert the authorities of overseas S-61N operators to this problem. (Made 24 November 1988).

4.22 Require, for UK public transport S-61N helicopters, measures to ensure that satisfactory separation of the fuel pressure transmitter hoses from adjacent structure and components is maintained. (Made 24 November 1988).

4.23 Require a review of S-61N engine bay firewall integrity, to ensure that significant gaps in the fireseal arrangement at the points where the engine mounting rear support assembly tubes pass through the canted firewalls are eliminated when the aft cowls are closed. (Made 14 April 1989).

4.24 Require measures to improve S-61N engine bay firewall integrity by blanking the inspection hole in each engine mounting rear support assembly tube. (Made 14 April 1989).

4.25 Review the fire protection provision needs of helicopter main gearbox bays, including the fitment of thermal isolation means, fire detection and extinguishing systems, and flammable fluid shut-off systems. (Made 21 November 1989).

4.26 Require that the S-61N rotor brake maintenance and overhaul documentation be thoroughly reviewed and errors and sources of confusion eliminated. (Made 21 November 1989).

4.27 Require that the design of the S-61N rotor brake torqueless grip modification be reviewed. (Made 21 November 1989).

The Civil Aviation Authority's response to these Safety Recommendations is contained in CAA Follow-Up Action on Accident Reports (FACTAR) No. 3/90, to be published coincident with this Report.

E J TRIMBLE
Principal Inspector of Air Accidents
Air Accidents Investigation Branch
July 1990

Appendix 1

AIRCRAFT GENERAL LAYOUT

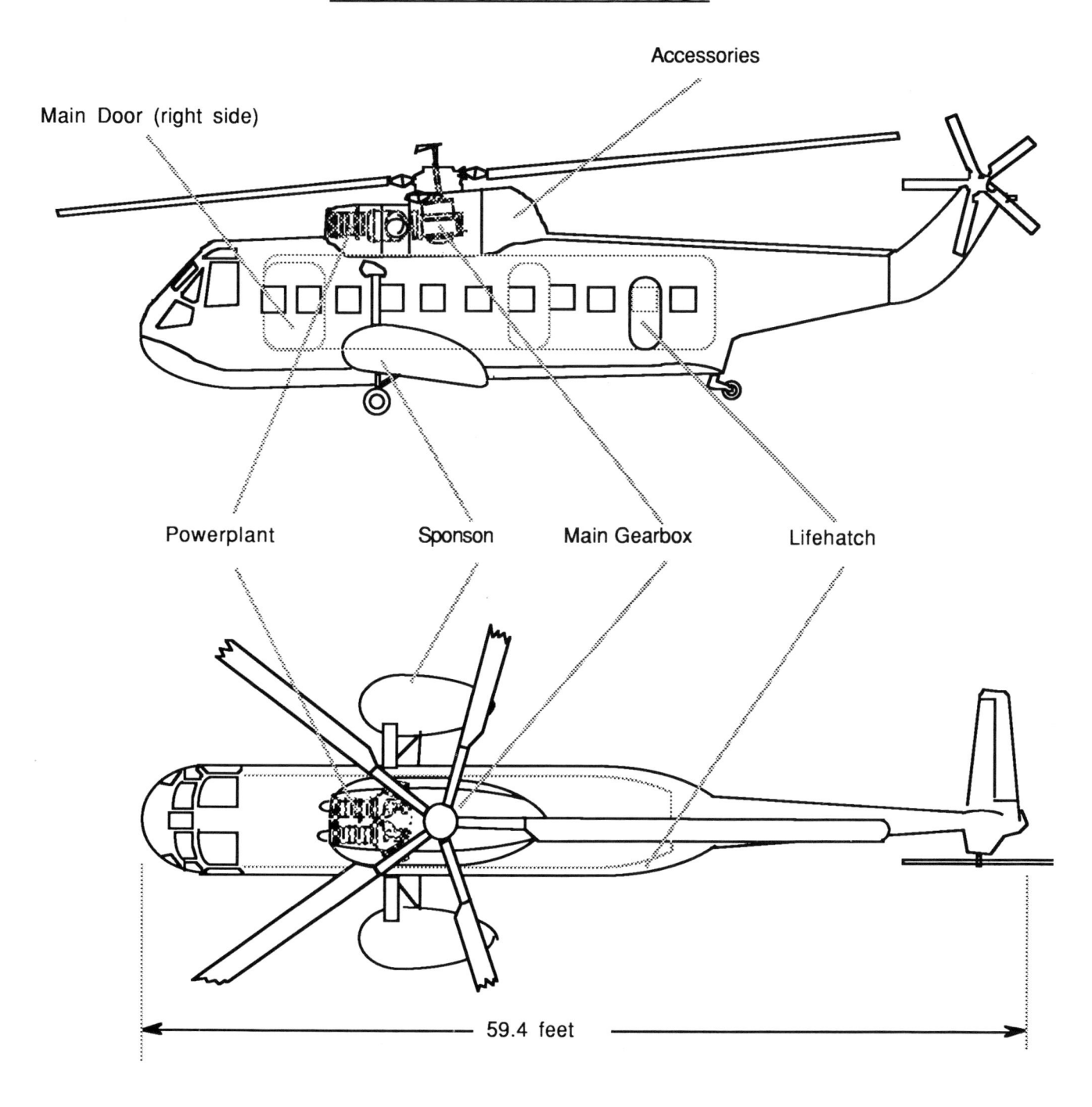

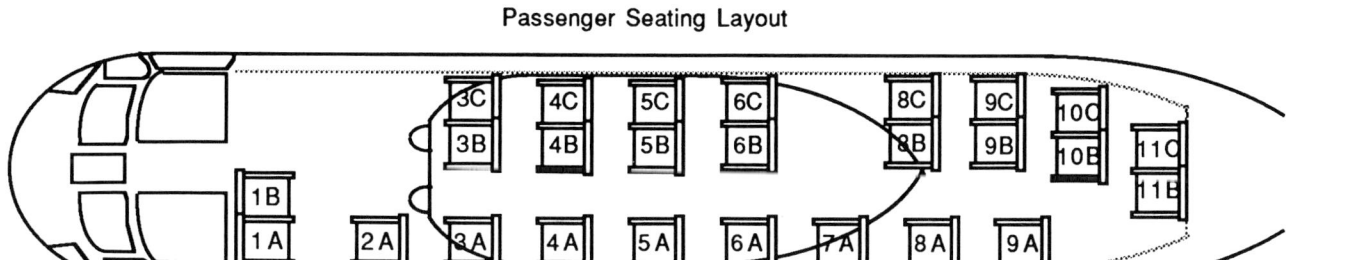

Accessories

Main Door (right side)

Powerplant   Sponson   Main Gearbox   Lifehatch

59.4 feet

Passenger Seating Layout

Appendix 2

POWERPLANT AND MAIN GEARBOX LAYOUT

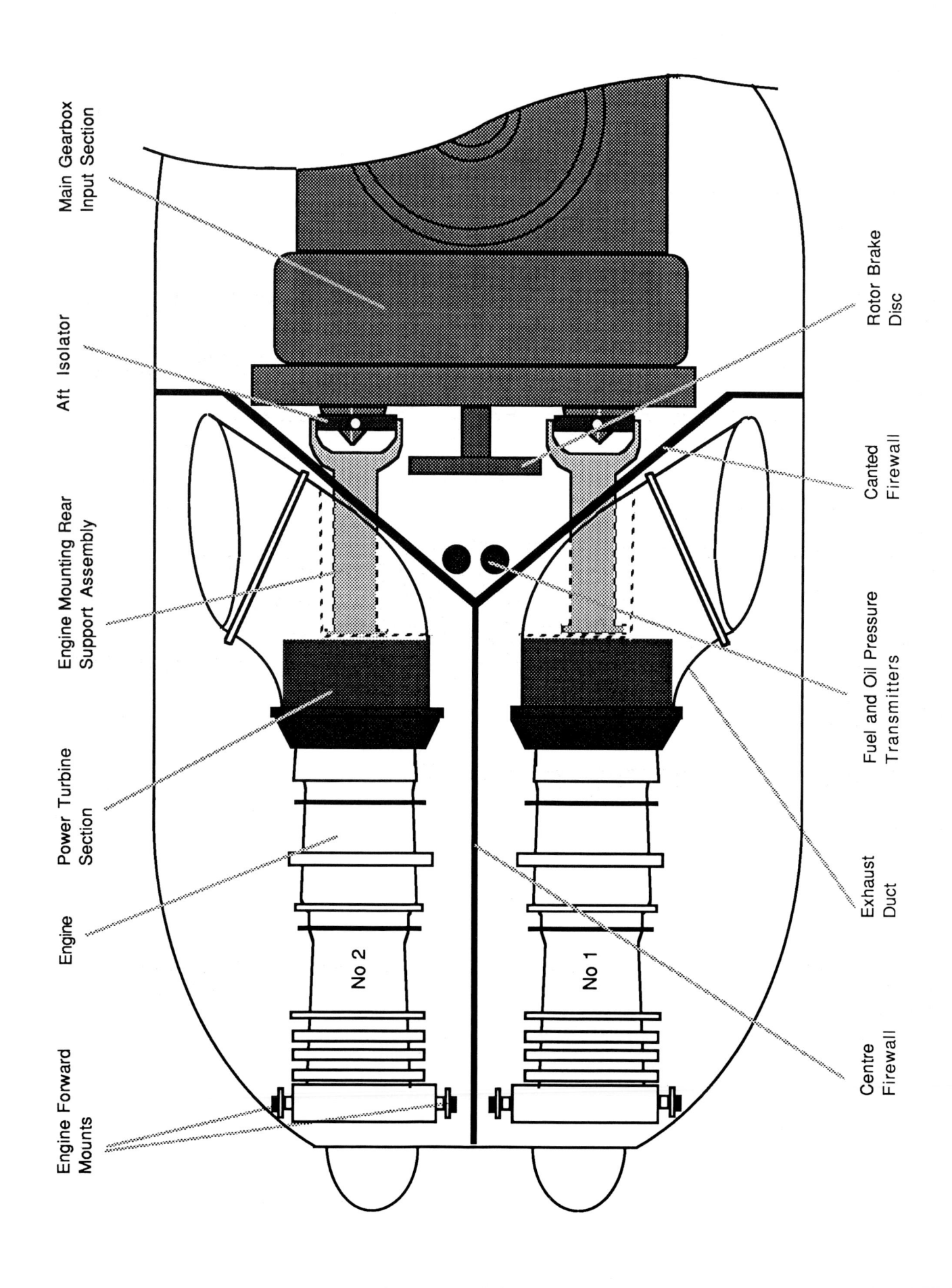

- Main Gearbox Input Section
- Aft Isolator
- Engine Mounting Rear Support Assembly
- Power Turbine Section
- Engine
- Engine Forward Mounts
- Rotor Brake Disc
- Canted Firewall
- Fuel and Oil Pressure Transmitters
- Exhaust Duct
- Centre Firewall

No 2

No 1

POWER TURBINE LAYOUT

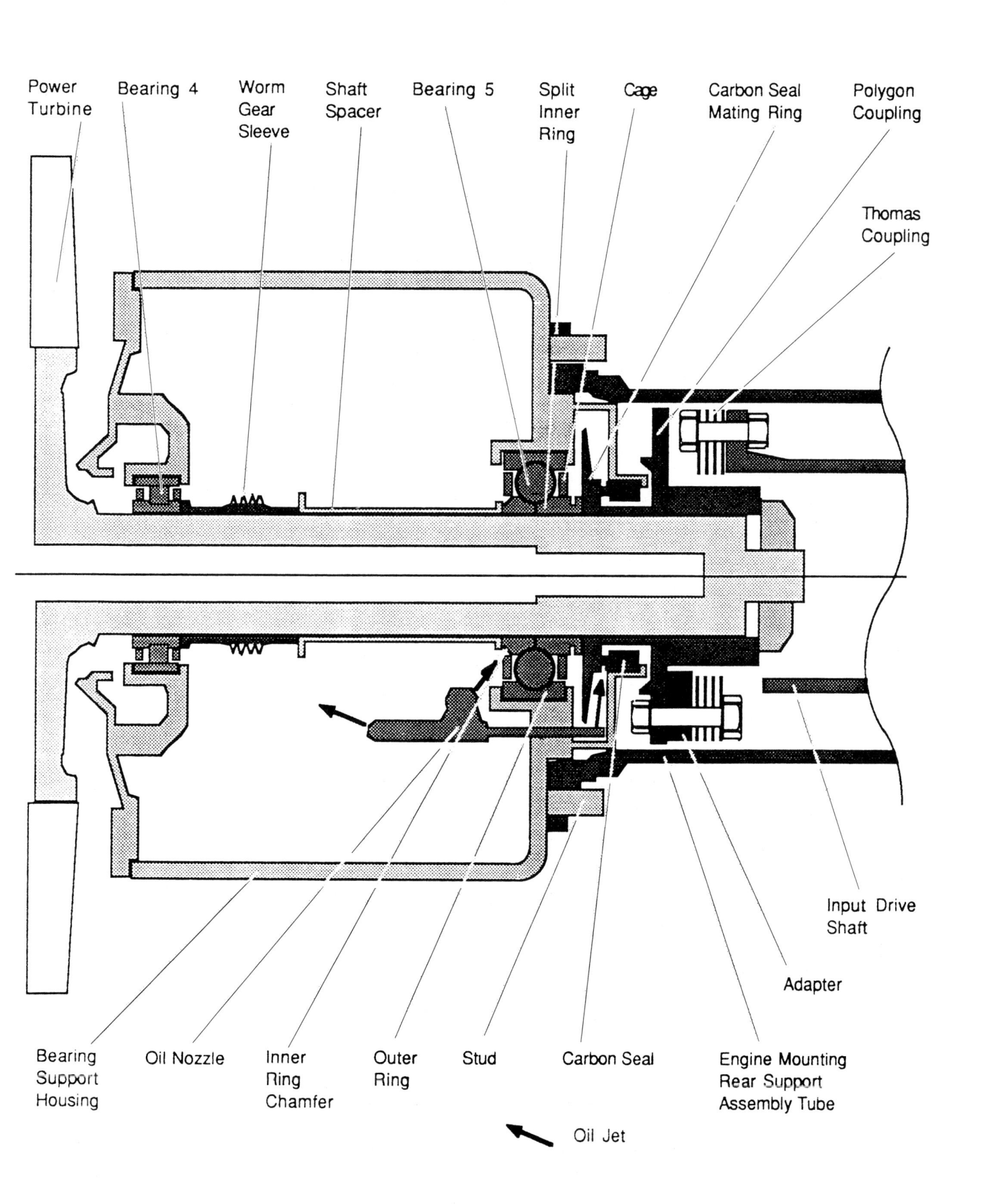

Appendix 3

DRIVE TRAIN LAYOUT

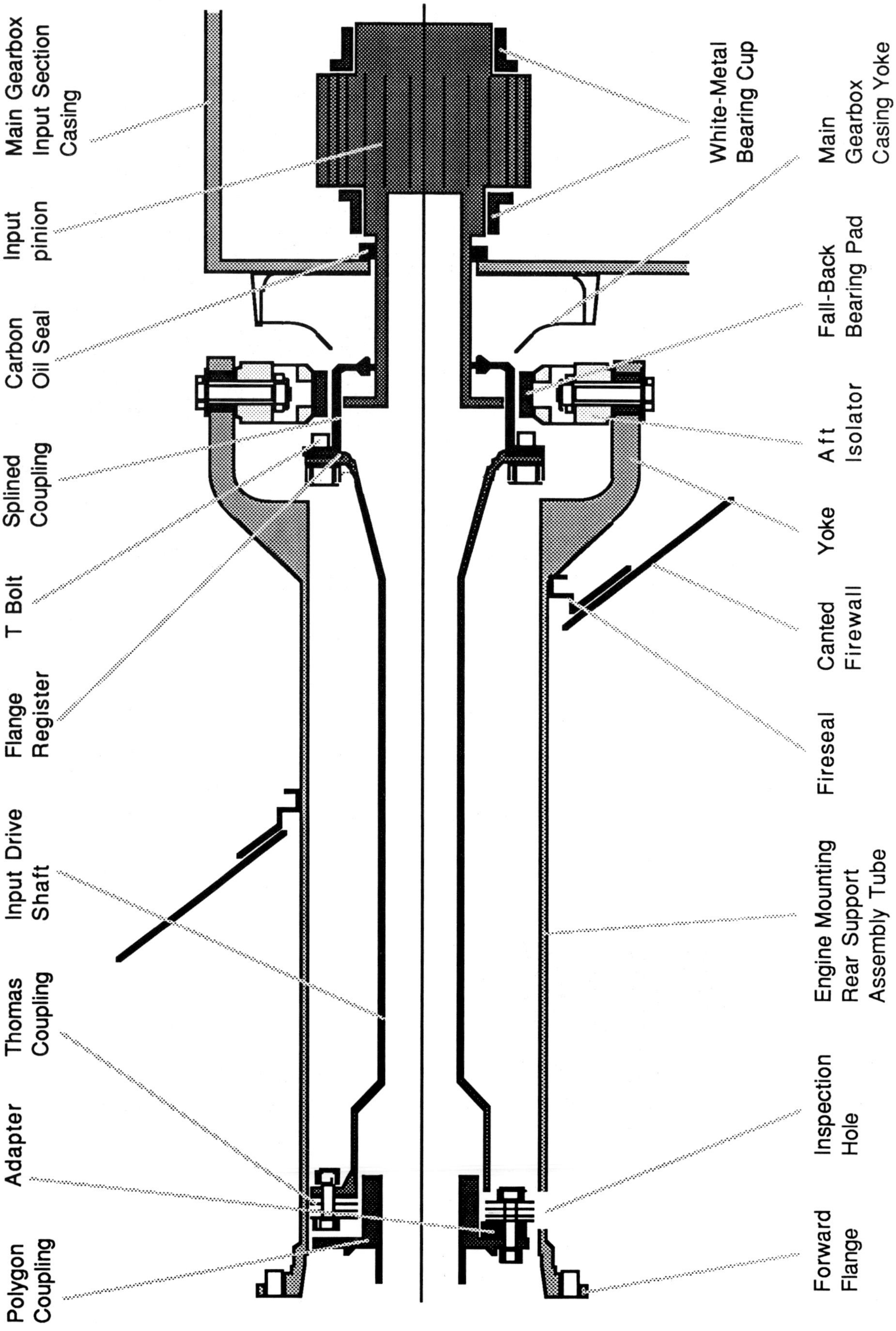
Main Gearbox Input Section Casing
Input pinion
Carbon Oil Seal
Splined Coupling
T Bolt
Flange Register
Input Drive Shaft
Thomas Coupling
Adapter
Polygon Coupling
White-Metal Bearing Cup
Main Gearbox Casing Yoke
Fall-Back Bearing Pad
Aft Isolator
Yoke
Canted Firewall
Fireseal
Engine Mounting Rear Support Assembly Tube
Inspection Hole
Forward Flange

ROTOR BRAKE ASSEMBLY

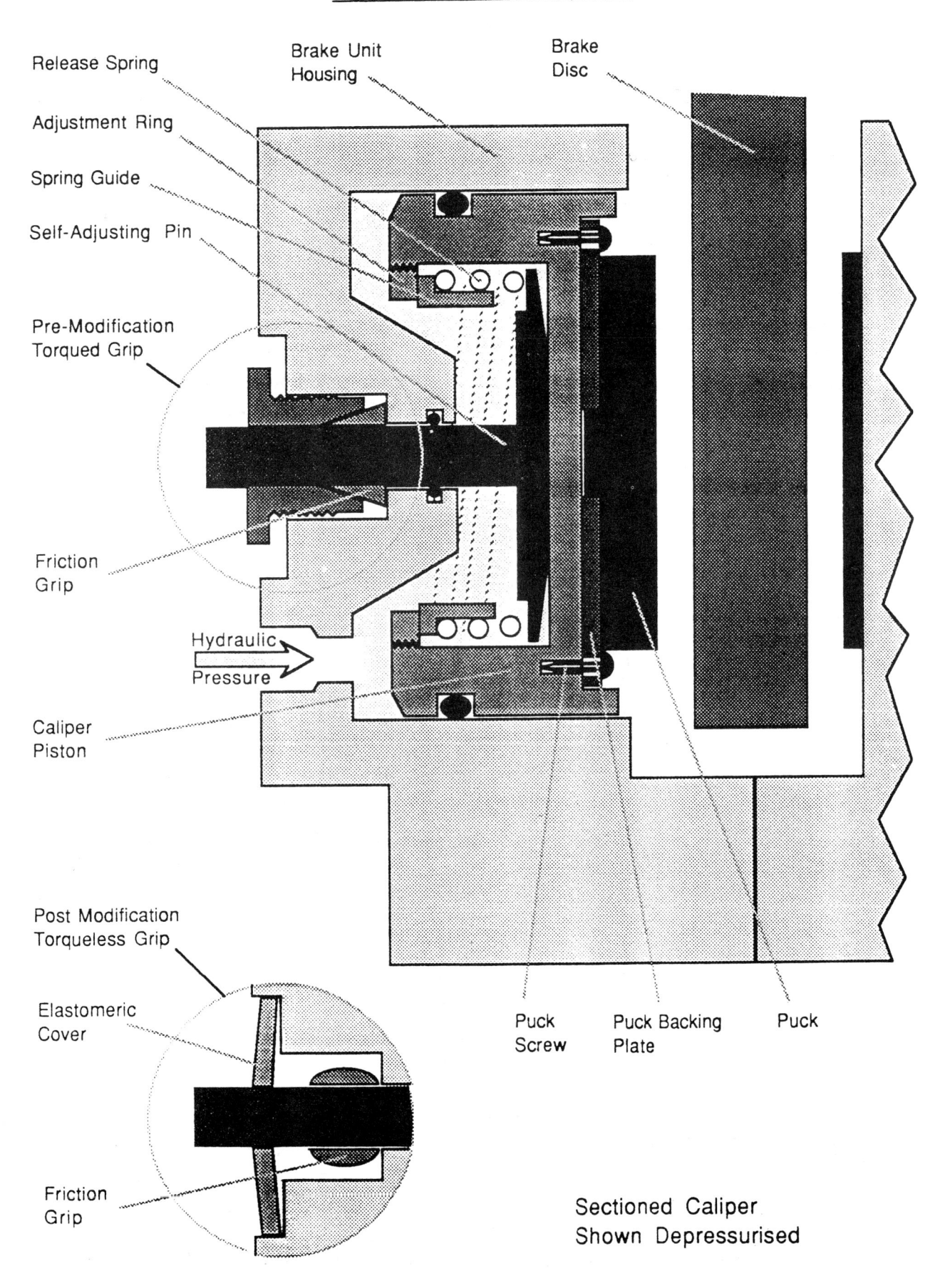

Appendix 5

- Release Spring
- Adjustment Ring
- Spring Guide
- Self-Adjusting Pin
- Pre-Modification Torqued Grip
- Friction Grip
- Hydraulic Pressure
- Caliper Piston
- Brake Unit Housing
- Brake Disc
- Puck Screw
- Puck Backing Plate
- Puck

- Post Modification Torqueless Grip
- Elastomeric Cover
- Friction Grip

Sectioned Caliper Shown Depressurised

ROTOR BRAKE DEFICIENCIES

APPENDIX 6

A)   Loose puck screws

Puck screws specified for the original standard of the brake, PN 944034, were type NK 526-632-5, 7.8mm long. Goodyear Service Bulletin (SB) S61-32-2, Rev 0, issue date 20 September 1985, and Sikorsky Customer Service Notice (CSN) S35-5, issue date 22 June 1986, modifying the brake to asbestos-free puck standard (PN 9440345-1), and to torqueless grip standard (PN 9440345-2) specified 9mm long NAS 1190-06P6 type screws but without requiring the screw holes in the pistons to be deepened. Rev 1 of SB S61-32-3, issue date 30 June 1986, corrected the error by specifying 7.8mm long -5 screws. This was followed by SB S61-32-2, issue date 28 November 1986, which required 9mm long -06P6 screws in conjunction with deepening of piston screw holes and a change in piston PN, incorporation of which was advised by Sikorsky CSN S35-5, Rev A, issue date 2 March 1987. However, neither SB S61-32-3 nor CSN S35-5, Rev A, required a change to the brake unit PN to enable units on which they had been incorporated to be identified.

It was also noted that an anti-corrosion compound was applied between the puck and the piston on puck fitment, which would have had the effect of masking any puck looseness.

B)   Caliper bolt/nut torque

No firm cause could be found for the looseness in the bolts and nuts holding the two halves of the caliper together, which was found in some cases, but differences were noted in the assembly torques specified between the Sikorsky Maintenance Manual and the Goodyear Overhaul Manual. The former did not specify a torque value in the section (Chapter 65-50-2, Page 207, Step 19) covering reassembly, and the standard values of Chapter 20 thus applied, *i.e.* an assembly torque, unlubricated, of 325 in.lb for the bolt and 275 in.lb for the nut. However, the Goodyear Manual 9440345 (Page 703/4, Para K) specified a lubricated torque value of 160 - 190 in.lb.

C)   Insufficient puck - disc clearance

Cases of insufficient puck clearance from the disc appeared to have resulted from a design feature of the torqueless grip modification, whereby the grip for the self-adjusting pin was not restrained from moving outwards (away from the disc) in its bore in the caliper body. This feature was unlike its predecessor, the torqued grip, which was restrained in both directions. If a piston were pushed into its cylinder during brake removal or refitment, or in the course of puck replacement, the torqueless grip would be moved outwards away from its inner stop. In this condition, the internal gap between the spring guide and the pin head, on which the puck back-off function with the brake released depends, would be lost following initial brake application. It was found that in this condition the puck would ratchet towards the disc during initial brake applications, finishing up in contact with the disc when the brake was released. Such an effect should have been detected by tests required after brake installation.